The Year of the Locust

The Year of the Locust

by
David F. Nixon

Beacon Hill Press of Kansas City
Kansas City, Missouri

Copyright, 1980
Beacon Hill Press of Kansas City

ISBN: 0-8341-0675-2

Printed in the
United States of America

Permission to quote from the following copyrighted versions is acknowledged with appreciation:

The Holy Bible, The New International Version (NIV), copyright © 1978 by the New York International Bible Society.

The Living Bible (TLB) © 1971 by Tyndale House Publishers, Wheaton, Ill.

The New Testament in Modern English, Revised Edition © J. B. Phillips 1958, 1960, 1972. By permission of the Macmillan Publishing Co., Inc.

Dedication

To my father,
Clifton B. Nixon,
whose godly life
has been a constant source
of inspiration

Contents

Preface 9

Acknowledgments 10

1. *Rendezvous with Truth* 11
    Pressures Need Promises 13
    The Thrill of Discovery 17

2. *Ready or Not* 20
    Spiritual Preparation 21
    Dare to Be Different 22
    A New Estrangement 23
    An Engagement Very Difficult 24
    Emotional Preparation 26
    A Realistic Self-image 27
    Overcoming Inferiority 28
    Life's Preparation 29

3. *Spiritual Leadership in a Locust Year* 32
    Compromise or Confrontation 33
    Conflict and Commitments 34
    God's or Man's Call 39
    Action or Reaction 40
    Leadership Costs 41

4. *Wounds of the Spirit* 45
    Common Emotional Disturbances 47
    Sources of Stress 50
    Understanding Depression 53
    Coping with Emotional Pain 57
    The Therapy of Prayer 59
    The Reeducation of Self 61

5. *The Modern Family Predicament*   64
   Moral Upheaval   66
      The Example of Noah   66
      Some Telling Statistics   67
      The Sexual Revolution   71
      Proliferating Promiscuity   72
      Sex Addiction   73
      The Fun Morality   74
   Rapid Social Change   74
      Reversal of Sexual Roles   75
      Temporary Marriage   75
      Life-modifying Sciences   76
      Technological Explosion   77
      High Mobility   77
      Urbanization   78
      Working Women   79
      The Future of the Family   79

6. *Locusts in the Church*   83
      An Unfortunate Atmosphere   84
      Understanding Differences   86
      Charismania   87
      Importance of Sound Doctrine   91
      Psychological Considerations   91
      Demonic Counterfeits   94
      Failure to Compromise   96

7. *Morals and the Media*   97
      A Difficult Inquiry   99
      TV's Impact on National Character   100
      Adverse Effects   101
      Conflicting Values   102

8. *All Them All Things*   109
      Job's Predicament   110
      Paul's Sufferings   112

      Perplexed, but Not Despairing   113
      Riddles in the World   113
      People Puzzles   114
      Heaven's Laboratory   117

9. *Survival of the Faithful*   119
    The Watergate Example   120
    The Andes Survivors   121
    Survival of the Faithful   122
      Don't Think of It as Punishment   124
      Refuse to Isolate   126
      Maintain Faith   127
      Try Never Giving Up   130
      Live Dangerously Faithful   132

Reference Notes   134

Preface

This is a book about locusts and locust years. Not the creeping, crawling, cutting kind of the insect world which devour crops and dreams and lands. Rather the locust type experiences of life and living which wound and wilt and wrench not only people, but also homes, and harvests, and churches. The result of their coming is always the same. There is devastation, loss, and sometimes despair.

How does a person prepare for a locust year? Who should expect one? Suppose I'm one of those persons trying to survive one right now. What am I to do? Why? Why do they come? These are the puzzles and riddles of life which make no sense whatsoever. Who's at fault? What did I do to deserve this? Why is God punishing me? What has God promised?

It is a book about restoration—God's promise amidst setbacks, suffering, sorrow. There is grace sufficient for any experience of anguish, adversity, or adversary. It's about survival, making it, coping, and learning to cope when one finds himself on the tangled thread side of God's providences.

The purpose of this book is to define a locust year experience from several different perspectives. I hope to explore the promise, the preparation for, and the process of restoration in a locust year. I hope to look at some of the areas where locusts have eaten their fill in the emotions, in our families and homes, in the church and in our morality. We need to be reminded that there is a way to survive the locust years. Joel 2:25 is a promise whose day has come.

Acknowledgments

I want to thank Karen Dean for her encouragement to start this writing project.

My thanks also goes to Ann Orchowski who typed the manuscript.

David F. Nixon

/1

RENDEZVOUS WITH TRUTH

It has always been interesting how believers manage to miss so much more truth by oversight than they absorb by concentration. For example, whenever the Book of Joel is mentioned, most avid Bible readers immediately recall that famous Pentecostal promise from chapter 2. Its fulfillment was realized in another significant second chapter, Acts 2:16. For most people, that promise represents the sum total of Joel's contribution to God's revelation. It is a beautiful promise to be sure. Every Spirit-filled believer has revelled in the glory of its fulfillment. To read it and catch its meaning is a thrilling experience. Reflection on Joel's promise still rivets one's attention:

> And it shall come to pass afterward, that I will pour out my spirit upon all flesh; and your sons and your daughters shall prophesy, your old men shall

dream dreams, your young men shall see visions: and also upon the servants and upon the handmaids in those days will I pour out my spirit (Joel 2:28-29).

This promise has always been held in the highest esteem among believers not only for its dispensational significance, but also for its prophetic fulfillment and its individual reality. No one has ever seriously doubted the significance of that eventful Pentecost Day, when after 10 days of prayer and anticipation, the 120 received the promised outpouring for which they had been commanded to wait. Often overlooked is a little verse nestled in the three verses before this exciting promise of the Spirit. Like a tiny acorn lying beneath the shadow of a mighty oak tree, it was packed with as much life and potential as the full-grown, now fulfilled promise, but not recognizably significant enough to receive much attention.

As one reads his Bible with close scrutiny, he soon discovers that throughout God's Word there are numerous nuggets of truth, often hidden from view, until crises and real-life pressures and circumstances cause them to be unearthed. Sometimes one must dig to find them, but they are there just the same. At times one comes upon such truths through casual reading. Either way, these tiny gems of truth have profound significance when they speak so clearly and cogently to specific needs. Many more are there for the taking, if one will muster the courage to search the Scriptures to find them. Strangely enough, the significance of many beautiful Bible truths is obscured until a real life need exposes an applicable promise.

Many of these undiscovered gems are gyroscopic in nature. The gyroscope is an amazing device used to keep moving ships and airplanes level. The principle is the same whether the gyroscope is found on a jumbo jetliner or on a single-engine airplane. When the aircraft tilts off center, the gyroscopic instrument on the panel indicates that some corrective measure must be taken. God's Word is filled with nuggets of truth designed to keep us on keel. When some corrective measure needs to be taken, or some adjustment must be made in our thinking, or even our faith, then these truths signal what must be done. There are times when all of us need that kind of promise, some new ray of spiritual light to burst over our soul, some new truth to shake us, or even some gyroscopic adjustment to get us back to normal.

PRESSURES NEED PROMISES

Many weary Christians, bearing the stress and strain of real life pressures, have found themselves in that deflated condition which Annie Johnson Flint described so vividly when she penned,

When we have exhausted our store of endurance,
When our strength has failed ere the day is half done,
When we reach the end of our hoarded resources,
Our Father's full giving has only begun.[1]

Emotions and faith can become so jostled and jumbled that one can hardly find strength to face the daily struggles of normal living, let alone the major crises. It is in moments like that when one finds himself with his back against the proverbial wall or at the end of his spiritual rope, that a rendezvous with God and His truth is most needed. Anyone who has not experienced those times alone with God in which His truth captivates his thinking and motivates his faith has before him the exciting thrill of discovery. That is the thrill of reading God's Word and allowing it to speak. If one is willing, God will speak so clearly and definitively to real life needs and situations that in the process necessary adjustments to faith will be made.

I made that personal kind of discovery several years ago when a previously obscure passage of scripture opened itself to my thinking and then to my faith and I allowed that rendezvous to bring the needed corrections. It happened at a district assembly when faced with the task of making an annual report which would indicate the progress, if any, of another year's work.

It must be difficult for the average layman to fully appreciate what a pastor experiences on an emotional level when he must report to his District Assembly before everybody, including the general superintendent, the fruit of a year's labor in the Kingdom. And maybe there is not anything like progress to report. Sunday school attendance has not doubled as hoped. Finances have not increased, and the budgets are not all paid as planned. Or perhaps this was the year when more people left the church than started attending it. But report he must and in that necessary process try to overcome whatever feelings of failure and inadequacy he might have. Defensively, the pastor hopes that no one really holds him personally accountable for the losses, but at times he cannot escape the inevitable personal conclusion that Satan prompts him to believe: "Brother, you have failed, and soon everyone will know it."

When God's work does not run smoothly, without incident, and things do not go according to plan, and a pastor finds himself up against it, there is a perpetual battle raging in his head and heart to overcome feelings of failure and frustration. To make matters worse, often frustrated laymen unwittingly, or sometimes knowingly, imply it or even brazenly say it: "The church is doomed under your guidance." No one will ever know until Judgment Day reveals its hidden secrets, the daily crises that God's men have faced; the burdens they have often carried alone; the heartaches and hurts they have suffered, all for the sake of Christ. I am not talking now about the justifiable criticism that poor judgment or mistakes have brought. Rather of those things which rip at the mind and heart when a man of God has done his best, but at times it seems that is not good enough.

Of course laymen face heartaches and hurts. Their burdens are just as heavy. Pastors and laymen alike struggle at times with feelings of failure and frustration, and the obviously personal conclusion that no one cares. But in a unique kind of way pastors represent congregations, and in the minds of many laymen the shepherds are expected to produce results, whether or not the sheep are willing to pitch in and help. The old "miracle medicine man concept" is still among us. The medicine man was something of a marvel in the early days of the West. He carried a potion that could cure about anything. In a similar kind of way people regard pastors as miracle men of God. Those who are successful in creating the miraculous are in high demand and have the greatest "marketability" for their ministry.

When it comes time for pastoral reporting, particularly when statistics do not tell the whole story of either success or failure, a pastor quietly hopes that his statistics will put him and his people in the best possible light. When that inevitable day of accountability finally arrives, it does not matter how confident a pastor is under normal conditions; when he is on the front row, waiting to report to his District Assembly, some strange things happen. His notes, if any, are crumpled and not a little bit moist from his shaky, sweaty palms. Someone always seems to be coughing, and one cannot help but believe it is caused by the stomach tickling his throat. It is really not that bad, but at times it is quite comical to watch otherwise confident men of God fidget and cross and uncross their legs almost in unison to the rhythm of their pounding hearts. And, of course, everything is funny, whether it is or not, because somehow laughter relieves the tension.

Then he is second in line to report. The dreaded countdown begins. Then the general superintendent looks over his glasses at the motley crew on the front row and utters the saddest words a reporting preacher ever hears: "Call the next, please!" Suddenly, he is on. His time has arrived, and now every eye will see and every ear will hear what the pastor has to report. Having cleared his throat, and taking a long, needed breath, he begins by addressing the leadership, if he remembers, then his fellow pastors, and finally all the delegates assembled there.

It is usually easier, if not more appropriate, to call a difficult year a challenging one, so that is the way most discouraged pastors begin. And since he feels that most people would rather not hear about his problems anyway, he tells them about as many of the successes as he can remember. Maybe it is because deep within himself he believes that his church really does have those "real possibilities" Robert Schuller says it does. Or somehow if he could follow Bill Gothard's six basic ways to remove conflict, it would turn into a miracle success story comparable to anything Wendell Nance ever told. Maybe he is just trying to "Norman Vincent Peale" his way out of the situation by thinking positively. Anyway, he begins by saying, "This has been a year of tremendous challenges." Adjustments sounds so much better than crises, so he says, "My church has faced many adjustments [Wow! If they only knew!] through which God has enabled her to emerge triumphant." Try to say that when it is all he can do to choke back the tears of frustration that he knows would surely give away the hurt that he feels. And triumphant? Inside he is saying, "Now really, who am I trying to fool?" He knows only too well that there are some deep-seated scars that might never go away. He only hopes that it does not show, for nothing has appeared on the horizon to convince him otherwise.

This particular report was beginning to sound a little hollow and disdainfully superficial by now, so he tried to be more accurate by quoting the words of "Amazing Grace" that had been a source of inspiration to him through it all:

> *Through many dangers, toils, and snares*
> *I have already come.*
> *'Tis grace hath brought me safe thus far,*
> *And grace will lead me home.*[2]

That was no doubt the truest thing he had said thus far. God had proven himself true to every promise of His Word, especially where He said to Paul and everyone who has ever faced a thorny dilemma, "My grace is sufficient for thee" (2 Cor. 12:9). With the confidence and support of so many in prayer, and the knowledge that God had stood firmly by him, he would have been remiss to fail to give God the glory, despite any feelings to the contrary. As he neared the end of his report, he gave his testimony from the words of an old hymn:

> *Jesus is all the world to me:*
> *My Life, my Joy, my All.*
> *He is my Strength from day to day;*
> *Without Him I would fall.*
> *When I am sad to Him I go;*
> *No other One can cheer me so.*
> *When I am sad, He makes me glad.*
> *He's my Friend.*[3]

The Thrill of Discovery

Having almost completed his report and being ready to sit down, having concealed every negative thought he felt within himself, that new ray of light suddenly shined;

that new truth he needed came bursting over his soul. A precious gem of a promise, hidden beneath the shadow of the giant one in Joel, mysteriously captivated his faith. God had uncovered it just for that discouraged pastor, but everyone present knew that it was for them as well. So he shared it with them that day. As he did, that gyroscopic adjustment started on his faith. The Holy Spirit began to lift not only his sagging spirit but those of all the exuberant pastors who were there with stunning successes to report and the discouraged with only their failures to try and conceal.

He could hardly express it, weeping for joy at the newfound adjustment in his faith, but he managed to reveal a formerly hidden truth:

> I will restore to you the years that the locust hath eaten, the cankerworm, and the caterpillar, and the palmerworm ... And ye shall eat in plenty, and be satisfied, and praise the name of the Lord your God, that hath dealt wondrously with you: and my people shall never be ashamed (Joel 2:25-26).

Of course it was a promise to Israel! But now it was an applied promise to a discouraged pastor who had faced a devastating year. He had read it, interpreted it, and even used it as an illustration, but never until that very moment did a truth so completely capture his imagination. It was his for the claiming, and claim it he did.

That there were locust years for Israel was not particularly enlightening nor helpful. Most everyone present was aware that the locusts come in various parts of the world. But never so clearly before, had the truth contained in the principle of the locust year spoken to present needs and personal problems. In countries where the locusts come periodically, they are feared and dreaded. The people warily expect them to come but are never fully prepared for their uncertain arrival. But when the locusts come, there is devastation and loss, famine, and even death. They swarm in hordes, blocking out the sun with an eerie eclipse of darkness and doom. Everything in their pathway is lustily devoured.

But when the locusts have eaten their fill and have done their worst; when crops and dreams, harvests and hopes finally lie in ruins, the locusts die. Then a marvelous miracle of nature occurs. The carcasses of these deadly destroyers, which have covered the land with a blanket of blight, now combine to produce a fertilizer for the soil. The soil is enriched and an even greater miracle occurs. When the farmer plants again, if he can muster the courage to do so in the face of all his previous losses, the year following his greatest destruction, he reaps his most bountiful harvest. The year following the disaster is a time of bounty, and blessing, and tremendous prosperity.

Packed into this sometimes overlooked promise of God is a diamond of truth for every discouraged, desolate, and devastated heart. Though problems and tragedy, heartaches and hurts often leave God's people damaged, desolate, and pushed to the brink of despair, there is a principle at work in the spiritual economy of God that will enable believers to muster strength and faith and the patience to proceed. In fact, there is no experience in life, however dreadful, damaging, and totally devastating, that need leave God's children destroyed. God has promised restoration for all the locust years of life.

/2

READY OR NOT

Everyone quietly hopes a locust year will never come. Oddly enough, some people make their way through life with relatively little trouble, aside from the usual frustrations and anxieties of everyday living. However, when a locust year strikes, there is seldom any advance warning. It is never really expected. The little failures and problems and disappointments may be handled as a matter of course; but when a locust year comes, it is then we are forced to draw from everything we are and from all that we have become, whether or not we are prepared. In fact, all of life is a preparation for the locust year. When it comes, you are either ready by virtue of character and conviction and faith, or it will knock you down and leave your life in shambles.

SPIRITUAL PREPARATION

I guess I was ready, though if you would have asked, I would never have been willing to admit it. I was raised as a "PK" (preacher's kid), and thankfully most of my life was relatively sheltered from much of the world's sorrow and woe. In fact, I've been a Christian for about as long as I can remember. To pinpoint the exact day would be difficult, but somewhere early in my childhood I decided that much of what my parents instilled into me through the church they served and the lives they lived, made good sense. So I stuck pretty close to it, though for years I could not tell you all the reasons why.

My faith was being formed in a home where love and discipline were given in measured doses designed to produce character. I never really understood how all those times I was disciplined for misconduct helped, but I know they did. I suffered much through the applications of the board of education to the seat of learning. Being raised in a church which demanded a code of conduct that the world would call peculiar, my earliest recollections of school were ones which often forced me to stand alone against the prevailing customs. In grade school while other kids were winding the maypole and doing other forms of dance, I always sat on the sidelines and watched, never really knowing if it was my convictions or my parents', or those my church had imposed upon me. Since it was easiest to blame the church for my convictions, I always used the excuse "My church doesn't believe in it."

I really resented it at times, especially whenever it rained. Every time it rained, the boys' and girls' physical education classes would go to the gymnasium for dancing. I would be the only guy in class who sat in the bleachers, alone, clutching to the note which read: "Please excuse David from dancing; his church does not believe in it."

Throughout elementary school and junior high, I had

many friends, participated in sports, even lettered in soccer the year our team was city champions. Although I did not understand all my personal reasons, my friends knew there were a few things I could not compromise, or at least I would not. I began to see that I could dare to be different and still have the friendship and respect of my peers.

Dare to Be Different

In this crazy world that justifies everything it does with the rationale "Everybody's doing it," I began to realize that I could enjoy many friends without compromising my convictions. Actually, to rationalize behavior by appealing to herd instinct is a ploy of Satan to deceive and destroy the last vestige of morality we have. John M. Drescher calls this rationale the "byword to hell." He is quite right to remind us, "It's rather revealing and devastating when all too late many times, parents learn that all parents hear the same words they assume they alone were hearing, 'but everybody's doing it.' "[1] He goes on to say that the real problem today is that "everybody" is afraid to stand against anything alone. And if more people would realize that not everyone has bowed their knee to Baal, we would take greater courage to stand up for some God-given convictions.

It's amazing to watch this rationale at work. With all the subtlety he can produce, Satan gradually chips away at our morality through the media of the printed page, the TV screen, and motion picture theater. As we read and watch and listen, we absorb so much that we become desensitized to sin and immorality. Then someone with a deep personal sense of morality simply asks why, and the only appropriate response is "But everybody's doing it!"

Immersed in a world that justifies even immoral behavior with this rationale, we do not realize that slowly, subtly, but ever so surely, our morality has slipped into a state of decline. Because "everybody" is assumed to be doing it, there is a kind of sacred sanction and an all-right appearance and appraisal given. Drescher says, "The greatest deception occurs when man tries to make group action a substitute for God."[2]

By the time I reached high school, my convictions started to become my own. I discovered that I was a witness for Christ who did not have to let himself be squeezed into the world's mold. When the world said, "But everybody's doing it," it was probably the thing I should avoid most of all. The world says, "When in Rome, do as the Romans do," but the Bible says, "Don't let the world around you squeeze you into its own mould, but let God re-make you so that your whole attitude of mind is changed" (Rom. 12:2, Phillips).

A New Estrangement

The sooner one realizes that this world is the dominion of Satan and that the current of society is not and never has been Christian, the better persuaded he will be to stand against all of it, even if it means he must stand against it all alone. Paul urged believers not to be squeezed into the mold of the world because the world is opposed to God. Harold Lindsell, in his book *The World, the Flesh, and the Devil,* has forcefully recognized the dilemma of the believer as a member of two kingdoms, Satan's and God's. He says that the believer's role in a changing society is to serve the world as a member of God's kingdom. This is the great paradox of the Christian life: We live in the world but are not of the world.[3]

The world stands condemned before God. Since it is Satan's dominion, it is in conflict with Christ's kingdom. The Christian becomes a member of Christ's kingdom by the new birth but must still live in the world. Living in the world calls for a voluntary refusal to identify with the world, while upholding the principles of the kingdom of God. Lindsell aptly states, "In a world that rejects not only these principles but also their source, a fierce war is being waged against those who own allegiance to Christ."[4] We are called to live in a world that is unfriendly to us Christians.

When a believer understands his paradoxical and unusual relationship to the world, he is better equipped to discover what his convictions are. Whatever Satan is, the world is; whatever Christ is, the world is not. They are as fundamentally different as oil and water, so that no union between them is possible.[5] I discovered early that I could not have the best of two worlds, Satan's and God's. And if I chose Christ, I must enter into a new relationship, not only with Christ, but to the world. I had to refocus my love and accept a new estrangement. As the apostle John says,

> Do not love the world or anything in the world. If anyone loves the world, the love of the Father is not in him. For everything in the world—the cravings of sinful man, the lust of his eyes and his pride in possessions—comes not from the Father but from the world (1 John 2:15-16, NIV).

To protect his love for Christ, the believer must focus his faith on Christ and spiritual things, not on this world of temporal things.

With a focus of love and faith which is in defiance of all that this world thinks and practices, a believer is prepared to face the locust years without piously regarding himself as a supersaint in spiritual aloofness.

AN ENGAGEMENT VERY DIFFICULT

When a person decides to live for God and His kingdom in a world that does not understand, there is a definite calculated risk. The daily taking up of the cross amidst circumstances often less than encouraging is to face what Cromwell called "an engagement very difficult."

The natural tendency is to withdraw and avoid conflict and seek the easy way out. But the reward and blessing does not come to the person seeking an easy way out of trouble; rather, it comes to the one who overcomes in the midst of pressure. The Christian life was never intended to be a life of escape from adversity; it is more of a conquest over it.

Harold Lindsell says, "Perhaps the worst advice to be given is 'Become a Christian and all your problems will be solved.' " The greater truth is "Become a Christian and your problems really begin," as long as you do not stop there.[6] The Christian must go on to overcome, not with some inaccurate sense of power, but with the humble recognition that he can do all things through Christ who gives him strength.

Often we think it would be a lot easier to be a Christian in some other place or in better circumstances among those elusive "greener pastures." Something inwardly longs for a place where witnessing is easier. My first year in seminary I worked on a loading dock at a truck terminal in Kansas City. When the guys discovered I was preparing for the ministry, they called me "Preach" from that moment on. It became a label I later deplored simply because they had a way of making it sound like a curse word. An eight-hour shift often became "an engagement very difficult." Had it not been an economic necessity, I would probably have found a more conducive place of employment. But the duty of the Christian is not to run away but to be a strong witness where God has placed him. As William Barclay says, "The more difficult it is to be a Christian, in any set of circumstances, the greater the obligation to remain within those circumstances."[7]

There is a vital Christian principle which is part of that calculated risk to be taken when one accepts Christ. God has not promised shelter from pressure, ridicule, or abuse. Jesus did say, "Blessed are they which are persecuted for righteousness' sake; for theirs is the kingdom of heaven" (Matt. 5:10). One night while loading freight in the front of a 40-foot van with my back to the entrance, somebody tapped me on the shoulder. I whirled around only to greet a pornographic magazine opened to one of the lewdest pictures to be found. My fellow employee was hoping to catch some glance of lust in my eyes, or to point a finger and say, "See, Preach, you're no different than we are!"

The reason why unbelievers cannot stand a Christian who is different is because they see the utter contrast of the two opposing life-styles. Perhaps they see what their lives could be, but they fall so miserably short that the only way to feel comfortable with the self they deep down deplore is to belittle those whose lives are different. Perhaps the nicest compliment the Christian will ever hear is, "Say, you *are* different!" To understand adverse pressure as compensation for the sinner's guilt helps puncture the balloon of persecution. There is no virtue whatever in allowing an unbelieving world to drag us down to a level contrary to God's Word. Rather, a Christian must stand tall and endeavor to lift the sinner to a higher plane where God may be found in forgiving love.

EMOTIONAL PREPARATION

Closely related to the psychological pressures of charting a spiritual course in an unspiritual world is the education and development of a healthy emotional life. A certain degree of emotional maturity is needed to prepare one for a locust year. "The years teach," as Bertha Munro aptly reminds. We may never fully understand all the ways God is teaching and preparing, but I am convinced that all of life is a preparation for things to come. Each piece has a part in the puzzle of life. Fitting the pieces where they belong is the problem.

A REALISTIC SELF-IMAGE

God used a very painful experience to bring me to a realistic self-image, a vital ingredient of emotional maturity and health. I was sitting in church with a girl my older brother had dated. She was blonde and cute, and since he was out of town, I figured no harm in at least sitting with her in church. Right? Wrong! It proved to be a total disaster and a very painful ordeal. I had learned to expect pressure because of my witness, but there was some additional pressure that I had not counted on during my adolescent years: pressure over the way I looked. As soon as church was over after the final "Amen" was said, I started out the door when suddenly he spotted me. People were crowded elbow to elbow, pushing their way through the foyer of the church, when right there in front of all the people who really mattered most to me, one of God's dear saints blurted out at the top of his lungs, "Don't you know red hair doesn't go with blonde hair?" Needless to say, even at the age of 14, I only partially succeeded in hiding my total embarrassment and humiliation. I had almost learned to laugh when people used to "joke," "I'd rather be dead than red on the head!" So I marshalled a quick, fakey smile, tried very hard to laugh it off, and quickly excused myself from the girl whom I knew did not feel that way.

I made it most of the way home disguising my emotions with silence and a gloomy stare out the backseat window of the car. No one knew my self-esteem lay in a thousand pieces back there in the foyer of the church. My parents couldn't see the crisis in self-confidence and self-esteem I was undergoing. When we finally arrived home, I went directly to my room where my real feelings broke through with a veritable avalanche of tears. My shattered spirit lay exposed.

Then a knock came at my door, and Dad asked if we could talk. He wanted to know what had happened, and I blubbered all over again, reliving the humiliation and hurt. My dad will never know the good he did for me that day as he assured me of his love and told me he liked me just the way I was. He liked my red hair, the way I kept it clean and groomed. He liked my personality and everything about me. Somehow, though I cannot remember all that he said, when he put his arms around me, I was assured of his love. I knew he loved me just the way I was, red hair and pimples, warts and all. Almost instantaneously I began to believe in myself again. I felt I was worth something after all. Since that Sunday afternoon, the uniqueness of my personal appearance has never been a hindrance, though occasionally some strange ghosts of the past appear to rob me of self-confidence and a personal sense of worth.

OVERCOMING INFERIORITY

I don't know why people make beauty and sameness the criterion of worthiness. Why must a person look a certain way to be accepted? Dr. James Dobson has looked at the problem and decided that our society has made beauty the gold coin of human worth. He says it is a problem that begins in infancy. A beautiful baby is a much more valuable human being than an unattractive one. This distorted system of evaluating human worth can be seen in a thousand examples. Dobson tells about a tragic incident which occurred in Chicago several years ago when eight student nurses were brutally murdered. The following day, a commentator was discussing the violent event on the radio and he said, "The thing that makes this tragedy much worse is that all eight of these girls were so attractive!" In other words, to use Dobson's words, the girls were more valuable human beings because of their beauty, making their loss more tragic. The logic is, then, the murders would have been less tragic if homely girls were involved.[8]

I recently had the privilege of hearing Bill Boggess, Sr., a converted drug addict, alcoholic, and convicted murderer, on life parole from Florida State Penitentiary, speak to a church group. He was not blaming anyone for his hard luck, he assumed full responsibility for the mistakes he had made. What was so compellingly interesting was the admission of a tremendous inferiority complex. He said, "I started drinking alcohol at age sixteen because it would make me feel bigger, a fighter."

He recalled one of the most painful memories of his life which happened when he was a very small child in the hills of Kentucky. He said he tried to follow his father from the fenced yard. "You get back in there, you little bottle-behind runt," his dad said. He went on to relate how that his father quickly forgot the cruel words, but how they burned a deep scar into his soul. He said, "I never forgot them, and worried for years about my scrawny body and 'bottle-behind.'" Looking back on his inferiority complex, he said, "I put several people in the hospital for poking fun at me."

The inferiority complex which created so much havoc in Bill's life is a source of painful agony to many an adolescent child who believes what cruel parents and peers have told him so often that he truly believes. Often the damage is irreparable and the adolescent feels hopeless and doomed. Thank God for parents who intervene to restore confidence and promote self-esteem. The only way to overcome feelings of inferiority caused by any number of internal and external pressures is to resolve to cling to a realistic image of yourself. It certainly helps if parents will love and support and encourage; but even if they don't you can start believing in your true worth as a human being.

Maybe you are one of those fortunate ones who has never struggled with a chronic inferiority complex. If you are, thank God, but please don't lord it over those still struggling. Maxwell Maltz wrote an interesting and helpful book entitled *Psycho-Cybernetics.* Dr. Maltz was a plastic surgeon who became very adept at repairing physical ugliness. He often put "impossible" faces back together again. Literally, he made people beautiful to look at again, who had become disfigured by accident, injury, or war. But in extensive research he found that many of the people who were made "attractive" still looked in the mirror only to see the same old ugly self they used to be. So he developed a theory that to be beautiful you must change your image of yourself. You do it by constructing a realistic picture of yourself and learning to love what you see.

Most of us will always be average, and we can learn to love ourselves as we have been created and not condemn ourselves to a life of failure and frustration simply because we are not like someone else, better endowed, or more finely equipped. If we can come to the place where we understand who we are, and not fantasize about the person we wish we were, we can learn to accept ourselves and be happy about it. There will be many tests to our newfound confidence and self-esteem, but the person who has mastered self-acceptance will gain more and more as he goes.

The first real challenge to my self-esteem came in my very first pastorate just about two weeks after I arrived. On my second Sunday there an elderly lady pulled me aside just before I was to go to the platform for service and said, "I don't like you. I don't like your hair." There went the hair business again! "I don't like you as my pastor. I wanted an older man!" Strangely enough, I was not as shattered as I could have been. Why? I had learned to accept myself and liked what I saw in the mirror every morning. Incidentally, that same lady at the end of two years of loving and giving, ended up saying to me before I moved on, "You're the best pastor I ever had!"

Life's Preparation

The preparation for my locust year was both spiritual and emotional. Through college and seminary, I became firmly established in my faith. I searched and probed through philosophy and theology and became thoroughly and personally convinced of the validity of the beliefs and practices my church esteemed. It was no longer the church believing for me as a spiritual crutch, nor even the faith of my godly parents. I took hold of a tested faith and planted my feet on the unchanging verities of His Word. My commitment to truth was firm. I rested my faith on truth that was not only theologically sound but experientially true. I indeed had a place to stand.

The emotional preparation came through a process of self-acceptance and assurance deep within of my own personal worth. Not a self-centered egotism that surely would turn others off, but an inner assurance that God made me the way He intended me to be. If He loved me, I could love myself too. Only later would I discover why the preparation of life happened the way that it did.

/3

SPIRITUAL LEADERSHIP IN A LOCUST YEAR

You cannot choose when a locust year will come, so it usually happens when you are least expecting it. Maybe your hopes and dreams are for the greatest year of your life. You know God's leadership has brought you to the place of spiritual leadership where you find yourself, and there is the accompanying joy and peace that following Him brings. A pastor may be in the center of God's will and be expecting one of the greatest experiences of his ministry when the locusts come. I remember writing in a Christmas letter the year before they came, of our hopes and dreams for one of the most fantastic experiences of our lives. How easy it is "to run out of fantastic!" No wonder Reuben Welch wrote, "When You Run out of Fantastic—

Persevere."[1] When the fantastic runs out, the only thing left to do *is* persevere.

COMPROMISE OR CONFRONTATION

Locusts appeared on the horizon shortly after I began a new pastoral assignment. Perhaps they could have been stopped if I had felt that I could compromise, but I could not. A substantial number of people held doctrinal beliefs which ran contrary not only to mine but also to those of the church. When the initial discussion began, I was told that the greater wisdom would be to preach things which safely bypassed the issue. Almost immediately I began to feel the pressure in my preaching. There is no doubt that God's man should preach God's Word regardless of its popularity, so long as it is bathed with love and understanding. But at times, in order to avoid conflict and confrontation, one is forced to live with the pressure of avoidance. It becomes a very untenable situation when the preacher must weigh every word or avoid using phrases and terminology that might be misconstrued.

Those entrusted with spiritual leadership do not knowingly seek conflict. Avoidance of trouble is always a good policy. While determining a specific course of leadership responsibility, it is a good idea to listen a lot, all the while praying for that wisdom James said the Father gives liberally to all who ask Him (Jas. 1:5). The scripture admonishes, "If it be possible, as much as lieth in you, *live peaceably with all men*" (Rom. 12:18). And again, "*Follow peace* with all men, and holiness, without which no man shall see the Lord" (Heb. 12:14; italics mine). Sometimes even in the waiting process the spiritual leader is committed to a doctrinal stand which places him in a kind of no-man's-land. You know, kicked if you do, and kicked if you don't!

It is a very precarious position in which to be placed

by leadership responsibility. If one believes that God has led him to the truth, knowing that for the most part his denomination embodies the beliefs he holds, yet knowing that he is expected to bend in order to avoid conflict, this can be a very wrenching experience. The spiritual leader must consider that decisions of this nature cannot ultimately be denominational. It must be a personal decision. For regardless of what the church says, or what advice one is given in handling specific situations, the buck stops with the man of God in charge. At times it seems to be an unfortunate corner in which to find oneself. Some problems, particularly doctrinal issues, do not just go away by choosing to ignore them. And yet to face them squarely and seek a solution puts the leader in conflict with those who disagree with the church. It is very important to know what you believe and why. This is no time for doubting one's beliefs and believing one's doubts. Knowing what you believe and why makes personal faith and commitment to truth of far greater importance than the easy way of compromise. In the crises of life and ministry only a personal faith will hold the spiritual leader steady through the turbulence that may follow as a consequence.

Doctrinal conflict is easily avoided via the road of compromise. If it matters little what you believe or why you believe it, then no risks will ever be taken for personal faith and conviction. But if his understanding of truth (doctrine) has been carefully hammered out on the anvil of God's Word, then applied to life and found experientially true, then God's man is not so easily swayed by every doctrinal aberration that comes along. This is why compromise by those on either side of any doctrinal issue is difficult. It is hard to relinquish your hold on truth when you feel very definitely you have been guided there by the Holy Spirit. Moreover, it is difficult to relegate your belief to a position of relative unimportance just because it happens to conflict with someone's understanding of truth. If you believe that the Holy Spirit guides into all truth, as He promised, then when He has led you to the discovery, He will not forsake you in the defense. Where He leads, a spiritual leader must be willing to follow, but he must be sure he is being led there by the Holy Spirit and not by majority sentiment.

This is not to say that once God's man arrives at a position he believes to be biblically and experientially true, he becomes dogmatic, sectarian, intolerant, or inflexible. It does mean that if the Holy Spirit has led him into the truth, that understanding of that truth is not going to be subject to change the first time it comes in conflict with someone whose personal faith and practice is different. Our understanding may change, but truth never changes. That is why Jesus asserted the trustworthiness of truth when He said, "Heaven and earth shall pass away, but my words shall not pass away" (Matt. 24:35).

God can bring us to a point of inner conviction which says in regard to the truth, "For this I would be willing to die." Few things in life are worth dying for, and most are not even worth suffering for. But for the Christian, committed to God's Word even from the earliest days of the faith, compromise was never a viable alternative. When Polycarp, the bishop of Smyrna, was arrested on Saturday, February 23, A.D. 155, the police captain pleaded with him to make the simple statement, "Caesar is Lord!" and be spared. The Roman authorities demanded that the Christians say, "Lord, Caesar!" But they could only reply, and be true to their faith and their Lord, "Lord, Jesus!" So Polycarp was led into the arena where he would be burned at the stake if he would not compromise his faith and make a sacrifice to Caesar. Then Polycarp replied to their futile attempts to dissuade him, "Eighty and six years have I served Him, and He has done me no wrong. How can I blaspheme my King who saved me?"

The proconsul became very angry and said, "If you don't, old man, you will burn at the stake!" To which he replied: "You threaten me with the fire that burns for a time, and is quickly quenched, for you do not know the fire that awaits the wicked in the judgment to come and in everlasting punishment. Why are you waiting? Come, do what you will!"

With that Polycarp walked to the stake, refused to be bound, and gave his life for the One who embodies truth. Legend has it that the flames formed a kind of room or tent around him and left him untouched. The executioner finally had to stab him to death to achieve what the flames could not do. And when he did, there came out a dove and much blood, so that the fire was quenched, and all the crowd marvelled that there was such a difference between the unbelievers and the elect.[2] The difference was and ever shall be that personal faith can never be compromised.

Truth as it is found in Jesus Christ must be worth dying for, else all who gave their lives for the gospel died in vain. But is doctrine worth dying for? There has emerged in our time of theological uncertainty a very novel notion. It declares with great earnestness that doctrine is inconsequential and that those who try to live by the principles of sound doctrine are somehow misguided. The important thing, it is said, is to follow the Holy Spirit wherever and into whatever He leads. The arguments sound very pious and convincing, but sound doctrine is foundational to a vital faith. Doctrine is the form one's faith has taken. It is the structure which supports uncompromising faith. I watched with interest the erection of a multistoried building. For several months, before the walls ever began to go up, the workers could be seen bolting and welding and riveting together a superstructure of steel beams and girders which were securely fastened to a massive concrete foundation. I observed a lesson on the necessity of sound doctrine each day that I passed the construction site.

The foundation upon which our faith is built is the Word of God. Doctrine is the structure or shape our faith takes—the beams and the girders. To attempt to build a building without the beams and the girders of the superstructure would lead to collapse. To attempt to build faith without the structural solidarity of sound doctrine leads to eventual frustration and disillusionment. Some may disagree, but I could never accept the idea that doctrine is unimportant without sacrificing my view of faith.

A locust year came into my life as a result of a faith and a personal understanding of God's Word which I could not compromise in order to avoid the pressure of conflict. The need to maintain sound doctrine made it necessary to take an unpopular stand. There is the petty refusal to compromise of those who think that in so doing they have a point to prove that is not worth proving. But proving points not worth proving is hardly worth it if basic issues and commitments to truth are not at stake.

Conflict and Commitments

A spiritual leader must grapple with the following commitments. First, there is his commitment to God who has entrusted him with the ministry. Second, there is a commitment to himself with whom he must live after all is said and done. Finally, there is a commitment to the church which has given the opportunity to fulfill his ministry within definite limits.

Decisions are made which affect all of these commitments. In my locust year, I did not want to fail the Lord who had counted me worthy to be called a servant in His kingdom, nor do anything that would bring reproach to Him and the Kingdom. Moreover, I knew that I had to be true to myself and do the right thing if I wanted to experience inner peace. Beyond these was an overriding sense of commitment to the conditions of my ordination. The night I was ordained, I was asked if I would uphold the doctrine and standards of my church. With a clear conscience I said yes and made a commitment I felt ethically bound to keep. I further agreed that if the day ever came when my beliefs and convictions set me in opposition to the church, I would voluntarily surrender my credentials and seek a church that agreed with my changing beliefs and practices. I would not seek to change the church to fit my personal pattern, nor inveigh against its doctrines and usages. Any decision that was made needed clearly to be the right decision, or else I would have been hurting at some point of commitment.

Decisions which involve the full range of commitments and loyalties are not made lightly without forethought and prayer. Snap decisions which involve life direction must be avoided. Some decisions affect everyone's commitments. Difficult decisions often involve destiny. The destiny of the church, the destiny of marriages and relationships, even the destiny of souls might be greatly altered. When such high risks are at stake, nothing should be done to prove a foolhardy notion, nor win a battle not worth winning. The right decision would be the only decision that counted. My faith, my family, even my ministry would be affected.

I have always believed that you do not have to win every battle in order to win the war. In fact, not every battle is worth winning. When the price is too high and the casualties too great, one learns that not every battle must be won. To forge ahead where angels fear to tread with no thought of consequences is foolhardy, not courageous.

Sometimes even with the greatest forethought the total casualty list is unavailable until the battle is over. Only too late we discover that hindsight is better than foresight. This is to say, one can lose sometimes in order to win. An occasional battle may be lost without losing the war. But where principles are at stake or where truth must be distinguished from error (isn't that the real war?) decisions have to be made by leadership that often mean you stand alone, hoping that the casualties will not run high.

In the light of my commitments, my decision was to stand with my denomination regardless of what might be the personal consequences. In terms of leadership I became the denomination in the eyes of those whose beliefs ran contrary to hers.

God's or Man's Call

The cables of my commitment to God and the ministry bore the strain of leadership at times. Stretched beyond natural limits, my faith persevered because of a God-given call. There are built-in pressures which go with the ministry that only a God-given call can withstand. When every external motivation to proceed is removed, a spiritual leader must rely on his internal and eternal motivation. The fact of a God-given call to the ministry is that steadying influence for turbulent times. Without it the leadership is not spiritual, and the determination to bear up under the strain will be lacking. Eventually the one "under the gun" may leave the ministry to alleviate the pressure. The beleaguered servant can find peace in the midst of the storm when he remembers that God has sent him out as a "sheep in the midst of wolves" (Matt. 10:16). Nothing else satisfies and fulfills like doing God's will even though the way is uncertain and the task laborious. To realize our being there is God's doing, alleviates pressure.

Spiritual leaders do not seek God's call; they accept it. God issues the call; it is His initiative. No one deserves a call; God simply chooses those with potential and abilities He can use. Often He sees more than we see. God calls, not the church. The church does not recruit its ministry; God does. One need not be abundantly gifted nor especially endowed with super ability; he must say simply, "Not my will, but thine, be done." God entrusts ministry to those who hear His voice and are willing to follow wherever He leads. When a man accepts a position of spiritual leadership, he learns to like the idea and falls in love with God's will for his life. God gives plenty of time to know beyond all doubt that the call to ministry is from Him. If the call is not from Him, by all means do something else! Sell shoes or insurance; work in a factory, school, office, or on a farm. Be an outstanding layman, but do not preach without a divine call! The inner call of God is a stabilizing, energizing, self-motivating force that forces the minister to go on when every external motivation is removed and circumstances seem to warrant defeat. In a locust year, it is often one's only hope. Thank God for the external stimuli which give additional motivation to proceed whenever we do not feel like we can, but God's man with God's call can lean on Him and move forward with the poise of His presence.

Action or Reaction

With a true commitment to God and one's call, a spiritual leader must then determine to act and react in love when faced with the consequences of his decisions. Here again is where the price of leadership is paid. Foolhardy decisions are just as costly as hasty decisions. Only the right, spiritual decisions are worth paying the price for. The spiritual leader should determine then that his actions and reactions are governed by love and compassion.

There are times when the only action is reaction, so it must be let go as a battle not worth winning. My father warned me before I ever took my first pastorate that I would have "to learn not to react" in order to be an effective pastor. That was a hard lesson to learn. It took a lot of bumps and knocks before I discovered the truth of his wisdom, and I am still working at it today. There are times when a leader could "lay somebody low" because they are clearly in the wrong, or could speak sharply in retaliation without regard to feelings and frustrations, but that is not love's way. If one must win the war at any cost, the casualty list will run very high. Some never learn this lesson and their ministry is ineffective as a result. A spiritual leader charged with working with people must learn this wisdom. Some of us manage to get along pretty well most of the time, but sometimes I have blown it bad and have had to suffer the consequences. It is still a good rule in working with people: learn not to react. Act, but do not let the only action be your reaction from the emotion of the moment. The person who acts and does not react is in control and can handle things more objectively than subjectively. Love wins the war. And you can lose sometimes to win.

Leadership Costs

Three months after my decision to stand with the church and thereby against those whose beliefs ran contrary not only to mine but to those of the church, the locusts came in hordes. There were resignations, losses, disruption of families and friendships with which to contend. Bitterness, tension, and discouragement were almost overwhelming. Opposition to my leadership mounted. Some were even calling for my removal.

I did not realize that the pressure of leadership had begun to affect my family until a crisis was upon us. My wife became aware of my decision from the very start and shared in it and supported me 100 percent. But there were times when she too would wonder along with me if that decision was right, or was this a war worth winning?

The pastor's wife shares in his calling whether or not she is specifically called. Facing the consequences of unpopular decisions is a part of the spiritual leader's call, but what of the pressure on his wife and family? Most preachers' wives enter the parsonage and take on the role of preacher's wife by virtue of their love for their husband. God leads in the selection of husband and wives, so indirectly He calls through her love.

Prospective pastors' wives should count the cost to be sure they are willing to share in paying the price of spiritual leadership. Pastors can shield their families from some of the pressures, but there is considerable spillover. If he is not careful, a pastor can unwittingly make his loved ones the brunt of his pressure and frustration. The greatest care must be exercised at this point, for it is so easy to do as the song says, "You only hurt the one you love."

In our locust year, Kaye and I determined we would not take our personal frustrations out on each other or upon the kids, but at times we failed miserably. We tried our best to conceal the problems of the church from the children. One day as I was preparing to go to a meeting, I discovered that we were not doing so well. My four-year-old daughter asked, "Daddy, are you going over to the church to speak in tongues?"

The real test of spiritual leadership is to live by the principle of love at home as well as out there where the people and problems are. The temptation to take it out on the kids or your wife, the ones you supposedly love dearly, must be absolutely avoided. If love cannot work at home, it cannot work anywhere. By the exercise of a strong will and patience, one can live by the principle of love at home. The ones we love deserve more than the anger and frustration we feel in the midst of crisis.

A real crisis came when Kaye began to feel, after many months of daily crisis and extreme pressure, that the best course for her and the children was to alleviate the pressure by leaving. Divorce was unthinkable to both of us, because not only did we love each other deeply, but divorce would have ended my ministry. Kaye struggled with a sense of loyalty to her children to get them out of an environment of constant hassle and her loyalty to her husband. We knew what trouble in the ministry had done to other PKs, and we were convinced we did not want that to happen to us. So, in addition to all the other external pressures relating to a doctrinal stand, the pressure began to affect my marriage and family. God helped us meet this crisis on our knees in prayer. If Christ had not been the center of our marriage and home, it would have surely hit the rocks. But with Christ at the helm we held steady, not only to our faith in Him, but to our love for each other, and our relationship was strengthened.

At times, depression became crippling, leaving us incapable of functioning at even the ordinary tasks. Did you ever have any doubts? Sure! I doubted the rightness of my rightness and the wrongness of their wrongness. There were events that would sting and hurt, and bring tears. The cost of leadership included bearing reproach for everything for which the church stood.

Then there were letters. Some were signed, others unsigned. One day a letter was placed on my desk which caused me no small amount of tears. For in addition to criticism of the denomination for its narrowness, I read the following forecast which I had only too often believed:

"The church is doomed under your guidance, and I don't believe any other pastor can pull it out of the gloom it has fallen into." Only later would it be proved how wrong was the forecast. At the time I could not prove it was wrong. I would record in my diary of events the depths to which my own spirit had plunged: "It seems impossible to turn the tide of events. A wave of pessimism prevails. One by one others are losing confidence in the church (and I assume my ability to lead it out of the difficulties)." Some would always find it difficult to accept the fact we sustained heavy losses for a doctrinal stand. The personality of the church had changed with a fruitbasket turnover in leadership. Attempts were made at every opportunity to build bridges. And God helped us greatly to do it.

Everywhere I looked there were locusts. Spiritually, numerically, financially, and emotionally there was inescapable loss.

/4

WOUNDS OF THE SPIRIT

Ours is a day of crisis. It is difficult to assess the effect of such crisis upon mental and physical health. Paul Tournier states: "There is a crisis today in every one of our disciplines; a crisis in science, a crisis in medicine, a crisis in law. There is political and economic crisis; a philosophical and religious crisis."[1]

Given this crisis-oriented atmosphere, is it any wonder that locusts have appeared in the emotional lives of people, creating havoc and despair? In 1972, some 8 million people were treated for mental depression in the United States and Canada. Of these, more than 300,000 were hospitalized. In addition, countless Americans suffered one or more symptoms of mental depression but did not seek professional help—because they either feared the consequences of identifying themselves as "mental patients," or feared they could not afford treatment, or believed they could overcome their problems without professional help.[2]

Depression is but one of the emotional wounds to the human spirit being experienced today. The heart of the problem is much deeper than that, according to Paul Tournier: "Man today is suffering from an inner, more or less unconscious conflict."[3] He cites in modern man "a muffled discontent with himself, a distress of which he is not always aware."[4]

"In every one of us today there is a deep uncertainty that stems from our inner conflict, from that separation between our spiritual and technological life," says Tournier.[5] The result is a world which is afraid. Without God, fear rules.[6] At least there is a national incidence of fear. For example, Harold Urey, Nobel prize winner and one of the physicists whose work led to the atom bomb, said, "I write to make you afraid. I myself am a man who is afraid. All the wise men I know are afraid."[7] Locusts have appeared in a world which is crisis-oriented and fear-dominated.

There is a tendency to think that believing Christians are immune to these pressures and the damaged emotions they produce. Dr. O. Quentin Hyder says, "We assume that because we are now possessed by the Holy Spirit, somehow this magically protects us from psychological or emotional problems."[8] The truth is that believing Christians are just as susceptible to mental illness as non-Christians. Moreover, we Christians sometimes find it difficult to admit to ourselves and to our loved ones when we become emotionally distressed or mentally ill.

All Christians have times when their faith almost fails them.

Who among the redeemed has not said or at least

thought the same thing, particularly if yours has been a locust year? We all have wondered at times, "Is there help for me?" Dr. Hyder also reminds us that "damaged faith can lead to damaged emotions."[9] At such times it is important to remember that it is not our faith, but our mood which has failed us. Experience teaches that these things, too, shall pass away, and tomorrow the outlook will be brighter.

Perhaps Sartre was right when he said, "Man is anxiety." It helps to remember that we are not the only person suffering amidst a difficult predicament, nor is our experience unique in the world. It is easy to think that we are the only one going through what we are going through, when in reality, our problems and predicaments are common to everyone. The emotional stress and strain of such pressures and problems often leads to psychosomatic illnesses. When emotional symptoms persist, they often lead to some physical malady. However, if the emotional symptom can be handled effectively, the organic illness may soon disappear making psychosomatic disability less likely.

This chapter deals with the subject of damaged emotions, not organic or physical disturbances. It is necessary to emphasize, however, that functional disorders (emotional damage) may lead to physical symptoms if not properly treated. A functional disorder is one which is induced emotionally, contributed to, or continued by affective reactions.

Common Emotional Disturbances

While the following list is not exhaustive of the many types of functional disorders, it is, at least, representative of the most common:

1. *Psychosomatic Disorders.* A psychosomatic disorder may be defined as a functional disorder such as ulcers,

nervous diarrhea, indigestion, insomnia, etc., which is caused by emotional or psychogenic factors. Such physical symptoms and disturbances may be the result of emotional stress and strain. Here it may be helpful to remember Dr. Hyder's statement that, "It's normal to be a little abnormal."[10]

2. *Hypochondria.* Hypochondria is an abnormal concern about health usually accompanied by the false notion that one is suffering from some disease. Physical miseries, aches, pains, and weaknesses tend to be accumulated. Such symptoms are frequently experienced among the elderly and retired who, along with diminished capacity and changing life-style, often find that taking medicine together with an exaggerated concern about health, attracts attention and keeps them busy. William B. Terhune, M.D., states categorically that "anyone who takes six medicines every day, indefinitely, is a hypochondriac."[11]

3. *Mild Depressions.* Some fluctuation of mood should be expected as "normal" for most people. It is that blue feeling that lingers for a while then vanishes away. Mild depressions may be accompanied by fatigue, discouragement, apathy, self-pity, a sense of uselessness, loneliness, and a tendency to see things out of proportion. This milder form of depression is not to be confused with severe depression which is debilitating and requires treatment. Mild depressions usually lift after a time, for which all may be thankful. In fact, Dr. Terhune declares, "I have never known a properly treated depressed person who did not recover."[12]

4. *Projection.* Projection is a psychological defense mechanism by which feelings, wishes, or attitudes originating within a person are attributed by him to persons or other objectives in his environment. The projector chronically blames others. He usually overlooks his own faults and shortcomings, and ascribes them to others.

There is help for a person with this wounded spirit if he will realize that everybody has faults and failures which may be freely acknowledged. When one refuses to blame others for his own failures, faults, and sins, and realizes that "no one but me is to blame for anything in my life," he will have a better chance of correcting his own mistakes.

5. *Eating Disturbances.* Disturbances of this kind are a form of neurosis. One psychology professor always told his college students, "The best way to keep from getting a psychosis was to get a good neurosis and nurse it to death." Apparently, many in America do just that in the area of overeating because it is estimated that one-fourth of the population of the United States is seriously overweight. Obesity is four-fifths psychological and can produce both physical and emotional handicaps.

6. *Marital Problems.* Marriage requires of all who enter it some extremely difficult adjustments which are usually complicated by some dangerous misconceptions and unrealistic expectations. A good marriage does not happen by accident and requires constant, diligent, and loving care. A good, Christ-honoring marriage makes for healthier adults and happier children.

7. *Problems with Interpersonal Relationships.* Healthy social adjustments are essential to emotional well-being and health. We all have an occasional problem in the delicate area of interpersonal relationships. But some persons suffer chronic disturbances in their social relationships which may eventuate in aggression, selfishness, faultfinding, suspicion, vindictiveness, or withdrawal. Such chronically disturbed individuals are seriously handicapped and ill as evidenced by sick viewpoints and interpretations. Social ill health and the attitudes which accompany it are often the source of actual physical and mental illness.

8. *Aging.* The difficulties of aging are physical, psychological, and social. While most of us are never ready for old age, and do not want to be handicapped by it, it is certainly much better than the closest alternative. Emotional reactions of earlier life tend to become more pronounced when we grow old. Difficult and unhappy old people have undoubtedly been that way most of their lives. Only in old age does it become more noticeable.

For the octogenarians, the practical advice of Olive Higgins Prouty, in a poem written on her 70th birthday, needs to be heeded.

After Seventy

Pamper the body,
Prod the soul;
Accept limitations
But play a role.
Withdraw from the front,
But stay in the fight.
Avoid isolation;
Keep in sight.
Beware of reminiscing
(Except to a child);
To forgetting proper names
Be reconciled.
Despite not solitude,
Let no one condone.
Cultivate interests
Enjoyed alone.
Refrain from loquacity,
Be crisp and concise,
And regard self-pity
As a cardinal vice.[13]

SOURCES OF STRESS

To understand the sources, one must first define

stress. Rolland S. Parker defines stress as a "very difficult circumstance or dangerous event, sometimes momentary and sometimes lasting for a long period, which is difficult for a person to cope with."[14] He continues the definition of stress by saying that it is "a change in the individual's world to which he is unable to adjust satisfactorily with his preferred means of adaptation."[15]

Dr. O. Quentin Hyder acknowledges that "some people experience anxiety without stress but the bulk of it comes from various emotional stresses and strains of daily living."[16] Given the inner conflict of modern man and the crisis atmosphere of modern times, stress has become the modern life-style. The heated pace of life today is certainly more stressful than that of a century ago. Urban life carries stress that was virtually unknown in country living. One need only open his eyes and ears to see stress. There is hostility and rudeness, and the selfishness of the crowds in cities. There is noise, screeching sirens, air hammers pounding, horns honking, hustle, motorcycles roaring, pushing and shoving on buses and subways—it's all part of city life.

There is the stress which accompanies poverty and making ends meet, with which the poor must contend, while the rich worry about investments and business deals and the state of the market. Others worry with unemployment and physical illness. In a word it is modern life and it spells stress. It is the wear and tear of life, but it is not the stress itself but the effects it produces on our bodies and minds that are damaging.[17]

Beyond these external pressures, there are a host of internal pressures which create stress. It may be a long-term frustration of basic needs, or an inability to express basic drives, damage to one's self-esteem, fright or threat of harm of various kinds from the world, or from trying to perform beyond one's capacities over an extended period of time.[18]

The following list of the sources of stress may prove helpful in understanding the causes.[19]

1. *Loss or Separation:* the death of a loved one, the break-up of a relationship, or extended separation because of travel, employment, military service may produce stress.

2. *Financial Problems:* The loss of one's job, unemployment, inadequate income, poverty, or anxiety over business concerns may be a source of stress.

3. *Mental and Physical Fatigue:* the weariness caused by hard work or effort, or unusual stress and strain over prolonged periods of time, without sufficient rest, relaxation, and a change of pace or vacation, or a weakening to the point of exhaustion due to illness produces stress.

4. *Faulty Self-esteem:* one's self-esteem may be deeply affected by a failure to receive recognition, unjust treatment, unfair criticism, or a failure to achieve personal goals, thus producing stress.

5. *Sickness:* Illness may contribute to fatigue, and particularly when it is prolonged and disabling, the loss of the ability to function economically or to provide emotional strength for one's family is stress producing.

6. *Overextension:* When a person attempts to extend himself beyond what his strength, intelligence, or emotional capacity allows, that overextension will produce stress often with disappointing and damaging results.

7. *Traumatic Experience:* When a frightening experience haunts for days, or even years beyond a reasonable time when it should have been forgotten and laid to rest, it may be a source of stress. My wife and I began to notice money missing from the house over a period of time. One night about 1:15 a.m., Kaye was awakened by a noise in the dining room. She laid awake

while I slept soundly. Suddenly she grabbed my arm and I awoke as a burglar on his hands and knees made his way into our bedroom. We screamed and fortunately he fled. Needless to say that was a traumatic experience, and for hours afterward we could not sleep. It took several weeks and months before Kaye felt comfortable sleeping in the house by herself. It's been over a year now, and it would be a little unusual to still jump at every strange sound. But such trauma is damaging to the emotions and if not faced squarely can lead to obsessive memories.

8. *Unresolved Conflicts:* When one is engaged in continual conflict, attempts to achieve goals which are too difficult, or seeks to continue a task beyond what his mental, physical, or intellectual resources allow, the result will be stress.

These sources of stress produce wear and tear on the spirit which will lead in turn to illness, fatigue, emotional discomfort, irritability, and other signs of stress which interfere in a healthy emotional life. Unless these sources of stress can be identified and relieved the pace downward accelerates to disaster.

Understanding Depression

The American Psychiatric Association finds depression "the most common form of mental disorder." Psychiatrist Gerald Klerman of Harvard University estimates that one out of eight persons can expect to experience mental depression during his lifetime.[20]

Paul J. Gillette and Marie Hornbeck have suggested in their book, *Depression: A Layman's Guide,* that there are three stages of manifestation. The progression of these is from bad to worse. The first of these is called *mild depression,* commonly known as "the blues." It is usually a reaction to events or physical stresses. It lasts from a few hours to a few weeks and is usually relieved with the passage of time or the removal of the precipitating factor. The second phase is *moderate depression* which is an extension of mild depression which may persist for months. The third phase is *severe depression* which is moderate depression that never goes away completely. Severe depression is longstanding depression which is not necessarily traceable to events. It is interesting to note that suicide is "the terminal illness of depression."[21]

Leonard Cammer, M.D., suggests that depression is not an outgrowth of modern times. It has been with mankind from the beginnings of recorded history. He relates that in the fourth century B.C., Hippocrates, the father of medicine, described the four temperaments of man, one of which was the melancholic (the depressive).[22]

We are gradually beginning to understand what it is and how to cope with it. For one thing, it is an illness. Speaking of the depressed, Leonard Cammer says, "Yes, ill, because depression is not a mysterious visitation of gods or demons, as many believed in ancient times. It is just as much an illness as kidney or heart disease or any other physical disorder that you might name."[23]

Rolland Parker defines depression as a form of extreme unhappiness, often combined with an inability to be active, and caused either by the stress incipient with loss of a loved one through death or the end of a relationship, inability to express anger outwardly, or lowered self-esteem after humiliation.[24]

Leonard Cammer sums up depression as the result of certain biologic and social forces that, in a complex setting, act detrimentally on the person's nervous functions.[25] He also recognizes the progression of depression starting with the blues which lingers on and cannot be shaken, eventually interfering with normal living.

All depressions are the result of increased tensions and anxiety. Sometimes the depressed is a frustrated perfectionist. When he doesn't live up to his own expectations he is depressed. Then the imaginary wars begin in which he thinks he is continually disappointing his family's or friends' expectations. The next step is lengthy self-indictment. Suddenly the depressed person is tired, does not want to be with others, yet cannot stand to be alone. Then deadly fatigue sets in and the depressed person has battled himself to the sidelines.

Depression seems to represent the mind's reaction, consciously or unconsciously, to rejection, threat of punishment or neglect, and to the mind's own ideals.[26]

Depression can be caused by any number of losses, or situational changes. Without doubt it is one of the most complicated and painful of the wounds to the spirit of man. Its milder forms dampen one's good spirits and hinder productivity. At its extreme it may lead to a determined self-destructiveness.

A depressed person has a myriad of mixed emotions with which to cope. He feels weak, hurt, tired, slowed down, paralyzed, unable to do anything, disinterested in anything but his own problems, hopeless, helpless, self-condemnatory, fearful that he may be unable to shake himself from the feeling into which he has fallen.

In some cases, there are medical reasons for depression and appropriate medical help should be sought. Nevertheless, most feelings of depression are based on how a person reacts to life's experiences. It has been established, for example, that some people are prone to depression because of an early experience of loss or temporary separation from their parents.

To effectively understand and cope with depression, one must first determine the cause, if at all possible. The causes already suggested are a sense of loss, an inability to express anger outwardly, or a sense of guilt. The loss may be real or imagined. The anger may be due to humiliation experienced for which a person cannot talk back. The guilt may be self-imposed reproach for failure to achieve superhigh, self-imposed standards of success. The cause must be isolated, understood, accepted, or rejected as untenable.

Depression plays no favorites. It affects the Christian just as much as the non-Christian. The problem with many Christians is that they have trouble admitting with emotional honesty that they are depressed. It is hard for one to sing of "joy unspeakable, and full of glory," when depressed. Some even think that admission of depression is a sign of unconfessed sin. Depression creates a burden to the Christian that the non-Christian knows nothing about. It should be underscored that hope is the antidote to depression. Who has any more hope than the Christian? Hope that life will get better in the here and now, enabling the Christian to experience abundant living, and hope for tomorrow in everlasting life.

In the midst of depression if the Christian will hold on to his faith with patience in practice, he has the assurance that "all things do indeed work together for good," if he will give God time. The waiting is difficult though. It can be a very painful ordeal. But as the writer to the Hebrews reminds, "Being punished isn't enjoyable while it is happening—it hurts! But afterwards we see the result, a quiet growth in grace and character" (Heb. 12:11, TLB). This is not to equate depression with punishment; rather to remind us that any painful ordeal we undergo can yield a positive result if we wait to learn the intended lessons.

There is also the therapy of prayer. One doctor treating depressed Christians said, "I have found that depressed Christians respond very well to the therapy of prayer. When I believe it will be helpful, I pray with them out loud, usually at the end of the session."[27]

Help for depressed Christians must not consist solely of spiritual answers. There is more. There are the practical issues of his problems which need to be thoroughly discussed, while appropriate encouragement, advice, and persuasion must be given in proportionate measure. False guilt must be distinguished from true guilt. Where there is unconfessed sin, it must be repented. Resentment and anger must be admitted and confessed. Any past emotional traumas must be understood. When this is done the Christian can draw upon the healing power of God with a confidence that God cares and understands. For as 1 Pet. 5:7 says, "Cast all your anxiety on him because he cares for you" (NIV).

COPING WITH EMOTIONAL PAIN

There are several steps in the coping process.

1. *Face your emotional pain:* Emotional stress and strain can be avoided by facing up to and accepting reality. This involves a willingness to take a hard, honest look at the things we fear. If we acknowledge the fact of stress and are careful not to allow our reaction to it to be worse than the fact itself, we will be better able to cope. Once emotional pain is recognized, one must accept it and adapt himself to it, changing what he can, and leaving the rest in God's hands. St. Francis of Assisi prayed, "God grant me the serenity to accept the things I cannot change, the courage to change the things I can, and the wisdom to know the difference."

2. *Learn to say "Ouch:"* With all kindness, but with cautious candor, when someone steps on your toes, say, "Ouch!" There is no particular virtue in allowing people to run roughshod over your feelings creating havoc to your spirit. When you say "ouch" it forces others to examine their own actions and attitudes and develop emotional honesty.

3. *Eliminate continual conflict:* this is to say, "As much as lieth in you, live peaceably with all men" (Rom. 12:18). However, if it is impossible to find reconciliation after suitable attempts have been made, the grace of forgiveness being in operation, do not expose yourself to continual conflict. There is no saintliness in butting one's emotional head against a stone wall. If a relationship is irreconcilable and only produces continual emotional pain it may be that the relationship will of necessity be severed. In its total honesty and candor, the Bible gives at least one vivid example of this principle. The conflict between Paul and Barnabas deteriorated their relationship to the point that Luke records, "They had such a sharp disagreement that they parted company" (Acts 15:39, NIV). Rolland S. Parker says, "It is emotional common sense to surround yourself with those who value you, who try to make you feel good, who forgive you your faults, who support you when the going is rough."[28]

4. *Develop other resources* which occupy your time, enhance your self-esteem, and build supportive relationships. Participation in small groups for caring and sharing may prove beneficial.

5. *Divert attention away from yourself.* Once there was a doctor in Maryland known as "the weeping physician." His beautiful wife died while still in her youth. The shock of her death plunged him into depths of melancholy and depression, paralyzing him. For years he was guarded by nurses round the clock. Plunged into grief he became an emaciated shell, having to be lifted in and out of bed, coaxed to eat, all the while detesting his nurses.

In the summers he was taken to the seashore for fresh air and sunshine, and one day the nurse rolled him in his wheelchair to a bluff overlooking the ocean. He persuaded the nurse to take a swim, which she did, not realizing what he was about to do.

She entered the water and he watched her, waiting for an opportune moment to throw himself from the cliff to the rocks below.

Then came a scream. The nurse, seized with a cramp, was drowning. The doctor, seeing her plight, stood up, walked without hesitation to a point jutting out over the water, and plunged down. Swimming to the help of the screaming nurse, he brought her to the beach.

He began working with her until she was safely breathing again. Need I tell you that was the end of his melancholy. In restoring life to the nurse, whom he thoroughly disliked, he snapped out of his depression, lost all desire to die, and thereafter found a new joy in living.

The diversion of attention away from self in giving to others is a source of coping power.

6. *Handle problems quickly*, whenever possible. If we handle them while they are small, they are less apt to gain emotional leverage over us.

7. *Communicate or burst.* Find someone with whom to verbalize your problems. Talking them through helps. Getting things off our chest with someone who cares is great therapy for a wounded spirit. Your husband, wife, a good friend, or your pastor is a likely candidate of concern.

8. *Don't neglect the spiritual side of your nature.* Regular attendance at the means of grace available and a strong, personal devotional life are essential in coping with wounds of the spirit. There is more.

THE THERAPY OF PRAYER

In his book *Release from Fear and Anxiety*, Cecil Osborne suggests three steps to effective prayer which are appropriate therapy for damaged emotions: awareness, acceptance, abandonment.[29]

1. *Awareness:* Honesty with yourself, God, and with

others is the all-important first step in effective prayer. Hereby one is able to get in touch with what he truly feels, to let suppressed or repressed feelings come to the surface. The Psalmist prayed, "Search me, O God, and know my heart: try me, and know my thoughts: and see if there be any wicked way in me, and lead me in the way everlasting" (Ps. 139:23-24). To suppress a feeling is to be aware of it without expressing it; to repress a feeling is to deny its reality even to yourself. Emotional dishonesty is devastating. There is no point in denying the reality of our emotions, for the feeling does not go away just because it is denied.

2. *Acceptance:* This does not mean approval; rather it implies acknowledgment of the feeling or the situation as a fact. It also requires emotional honesty. Denial of the realities of our emotions is futile. If unpleasant emotions are repressed into the unconscious mind, Osborne says, "it will simply fester and carry out its ugly work of causing emotional or physical symptoms." He correctly emphasizes that the "isness" of things must be accepted.

3. *Abandonment:* This final step of effective prayer means giving up the negative emotion or problem to God. It is that point of release or surrender that the Psalmist reached when he admonished, "Commit thy way unto the Lord; trust also in him; and he shall bring it to pass" (Ps. 37:5).

Earl Lee explains the meaning of this verse in a free translation of the Indian language Marathi. It says, "Turn what you are and what you have over to God—palms down."[30] He continues, "Suppose I hold a piece of chalk in my hand and ask you to take it. You reach out and take it from my upturned hand. But commitment means that we turn our palms over and completely drop what we hold."[31]

Abandonment in prayer is coming to the place where we release our grip and give things to God, palms down, fingers spread. The result of this process is rest in the Lord. When as Lee says, "Nothing of it sticks to our hands," we have abandoned ourselves to God in an unconditional surrender. Our whole self then rests on God and with an active exercise of the will, we wait patiently for God to bring us out.

THE REEDUCATION OF SELF

William B. Terhune, M.D., has developed a scientific approach to life which he calls "the reeducation of self." The approach began to be used in 1890 by Dr. Paul DuBois of Switzerland, who first assembled the reeducational approach. French neuro-psychiatrists used it successfully in the early 1900s. It was eventually brought to America, reorganized, and used for about 30 years by Dr. Austin Fox Riggs, at Stockbridge, Mass. Beginning in 1934, reeducation became the method of psychiatric treatment at the Terhune Clinic in Silver Hill, New Canaan, Conn.

The theory of reeducation is worthy of note in the matter of damaged emotions. Simply stated it is this: An individual can be physically and psychologically retrained in new habits of thinking, feeling, and acting.[32]

The process of reeducation involves:

1. The use of *intelligence*
2. The need for *an understanding* of self and others
3. The need to face *reality*
4. *Self-discipline*
5. *Practical idealism*

Moreover, it involves a healthy introspection for the purpose of gaining insight into oneself and one's feelings. The use of intelligence will motivate us to seek self-knowledge. We need not be afraid to learn about ourselves. We dare not withdraw from talking through our problems, our faults, our weaknesses, and our virtues with our spouse, with an understanding friend, or with our pastor.

A definite need exists to discover emotional understanding. Simply to know "why" is not enough. We must understand ourselves and others, avoiding emotional dishonesty and bringing our needs to God.

The need to face reality implies a willingness to dig deep into our past and search for those moments where emotional development may have been arrested. It demands that childish fixations be resolved, that prejudice be dispelled, that wishful thinking be avoided, that ignorance be corrected, and that one's world be examined objectively. Our refusal to face facts realistically requires that we face severe emotional consequences.

To overcome damaged emotions requires self-discipline. Though some of us instinctively object to the idea of discipline, it is desperately needed for emotional well-being. Everyone needs to answer to something or someone. Paul disclosed, "I keep under my body, and bring it into subjection: lest that by any means, when I have preached to others, I myself should be a castaway" (1 Cor. 9:27). We dare not rebel against reasonable discipline of the body, mind, and spirit. Rather, we must actively seek its help for our emotional welfare.

Finally, we must approach life with a practical idealism. When I graduated from seminary, I entered the pastorate with preconceived notions and ideals about how things ought to be. It took a couple of years to discover that life doesn't always go by the ideal. More often it doesn't. Idealism is not wrong, but emotional common sense requires that it be practical. If an ideal is a mental concept of perfection which may be approached but never reached, it serves to keep healthy goals before us. However, when allowed to whip us and defeat us because we expect of ourselves and others absolute perfection, it is disruptive of healthy emotional living.

God's grace is sufficient for every wound of the spirit we may suffer. If it seems that the locusts have swarmed over your emotions and there is damage, remember the words of Vivian A. Kretz:

> *"Thou wilt keep him in perfect peace,*
> *Whose mind is stayed on thee."*
> *When the shadows come and darkness falls,*
> *He giveth inward peace.*
> *Oh, He is the only perfect resting place!*
> *He giveth perfect peace.*
> *"Thou wilt keep him in perfect peace,*
> *Whose mind is stayed on thee."* [33]

/5

THE MODERN FAMILY PREDICAMENT

Ever since the days of Noah pressures have existed in the world to undermine the home. Serious observers of the contemporary scene are convinced that today's family is heading for disaster. David A. Seamands for one describes the plight of modern family life as "the American family tragedy." Others, like Dr. James Dobson, Jr., motivated by an intense personal concern for the future of the family, have written books like *Family Under Fire* to create an awareness of what is happening. Edward Shorter believes that the contemporary family is heading for the unknown. He says, "When Captain Video told Ranger to set the course for the heart of the sun, he thought he was undertaking a voyage that no one had ever made before." Shorter uses this analogy to describe what is the plight of what he calls "the post-modern family."¹

This voyage that no one has ever made before is directionless. It is characterized by a lack of clear guidelines and objectives. The coauthors of *Open Family Living* describe this directionless style of family living:

> Parents are often frustrated, upset, irritable, weary, dissatisfied, unhappy, unable to control their children, not certain from one day to the next what is going to happen. Treatment of children is erratic and inconsistent, sometimes harsh, at other times overpermissive. A family of this sort tends to break apart, the children going one way and the parents another, and often each of the parents goes a different way. A family in this state may not be much more than a collection of individuals temporarily living in the same household with little common interest in their joint future.²

It was once true that the family in traditional society could be thought of as a ship held fast at its moorings. From every side great cables ran down to bind her to the dock. The ship sailed nowhere and was simply a part of the harbor with all its safety and security. The contemporary family scene may now be compared to a ship adrift on an angry sea. In modern times the family has drifted onto the high seas, and the world of metaphor which such a voyage suggests started to fix itself in the vocabulary of social analysis. Edward Shorter asks some penetrating questions about such a voyage:

> Had the winds always blown so strongly as now? Had the currents always been so powerful, the family so little able to navigate a separate course? Was the captain's hand unsteady, or was it that the little ship was carried by such forces as capitalism, anonymous urban life, and the great tides of rationality and secularism over which it had no control? Above all, how was it that the family had managed to slip its moorings at the traditional dock?³

Such concern over the future of the modern-day family, coupled with unprecedented pressure against the home, leads to the conclusion that today's family is suffering a locust year. So many factors are in league against the family that even concerned Christians wonder if it can survive.

There are no quick panaceas or plans. And it must be admitted that being a Christian family in an unchristian world is not easy. The pressures are complex, the answers are not simple. No one seems brave enough to declare a viable solution. It will help to remember that the pressures have always been great both within and without the home.

MORAL UPHEAVAL

The Example of Noah

The Bible tells of at least one family that withstood the pressures of its day, and God thoroughly blessed them for it. Noah raised a family for God during the days of the greatest moral decay ever recorded. Conditions had deteriorated so badly that when God saw the wickedness of man, He "repented . . . that he had made man . . . it grieved him at his heart" (Gen. 6:6). At a time when every other family seemingly turned its back upon God, Noah's family stood firm. Apparently Noah was able to overcome evil influences and instill in his children not only a respect for the moral law of God, but also a faith so firm and strong that they all stood firm in the face of ridicule and rebellion against God and everything that was good and upright.

"Noah found grace in the eyes of the Lord" (Gen. 6:8). God told Noah of His purpose to destroy the earth and every living thing in it. But because Noah and his family found grace in the eyes of the Lord, they were spared. Can you imagine what Noah's children must have said to him during those growing up years when they had to help in the building of that hulk of a ship? "But Dad, no one else lives this way!" "Why are we the only family who lives like this?" In one sense, their situation was even worse than ours: Noah's family was the only one alive who loved God. There are tremendous pressures militating against our homes today, but at least we have others who love God to surround us and support us. Noah's family had no one, and still they made it.

Noah's family loved and worshipped God alone. They obeyed God's commandments alone. They built an ark alone. If the Christian family is to survive the current pessimism and handwringing going on concerning its future, it will have to accomplish it alone. Failure in our homes cannot be blamed upon anyone or anything else. If the Christian family succeeds, it will be because God enabled it to withstand the pressures pitted against it.

If a God-honoring family like Noah's could make it, and having done all, still be standing, what greater possibilities exist for today's family with the grace of God and the help of the Holy Spirit at our disposal? If Noah could raise a family for God and preserve his marriage during the lowest period of human history, there is every reason to believe that we are not fighting a losing battle today.

SOME TELLING STATISTICS

A brief look at the current statistics on marriage and divorce in America leads to the inevitable conclusion that never before have so many men and women been putting asunder "what God hath joined together." According to the U.S. National Center for Health Statistics and the U.S. Bureau of Census, in 1950 the rate per 1,000 population of marriages was 11.1, while the rate of divorce per 1,000 population was 2.6. In 1976 the marriage rate per 1,000 was

9.9, while the divorce rate was 5.0. In 1976 there was a total of 2,133,000 marriages, which was 20,000 fewer than the final 1975 total of 2,152,663.

The number of marriages was lower in 1976 than in any year since 1969. After increasing for 15 years from 1959 to 1973, the number of marriages declined in both 1974 and 1975. In 1976, the provisional marriage rate dropped for the fourth consecutive year to 9.9 per 1,000 population, which was 2 percent lower than the final rate for 1975. Interestingly, the 1976 marriage rate was 10 percent lower than both the final rate for 1975, and the 22-year high reached in 1972.

A total of 1,077,000 divorces were granted in 1976, which indicated an increase of 41,000 over the previous year or 4 percent. The number of divorces in the United States has increased every year since 1962 and has more than doubled between 1966 (499,000 divorces) and 1976 (1,077,000 divorces). In 1975 it could be said that at least one out of every three marriages would end in divorce. The 1976 figures indicate one of every two marriages will terminate in the divorce courts. One-half of all marriages are headed for the rocks!

This high incidence of divorce has created an unbelievably heavy workload in the courts. So much so that St. Louis Judge William M. Corrigan, who delivered a "state of the judiciary" speech to the County Council in January of 1978, pleaded for St. Louis County residents to stay married. Noting that the court handled about 7,200 marriage dissolution cases in 1976, Corrigan said, "We are all concerned about crime in general, and in specific areas with younger people about drugs and alcohol. However, in my opinion, the real cancer in St. Louis society, as well as nationally, is the utter disregard of family life."[4] He further noted that "the divorce rate is increasing at an alarming pace and shows no evidence of abating," and urged that the people of this county reassess their sense of values and reevaluate their priorities toward family life, and make firm commitments to honor the vows they so willingly accepted on the day they were married. "Unless families become more stable," the judge said, "crime and drug problems can only grow worse."[5]

Another shocking statistic concerns a rising number of unmarried couples living together. It has become an emerging social trend of the 1970s, says the Census Bureau. The number of unmarried persons who have decided to share living quarters has more than doubled since 1970. In a report issued February 8, 1978, Arthur Norton, who directed the study, said the phenomenon was not a passing fad. "This is a true, accepted social trend," he said, adding that he expected the number of unmarried roommates to increase even more.

The report said that in March, 1976, when the statistics were compiled, 1.32 million unmarried Americans lived with a member of the opposite sex in a two-person household, compared with 654,000 in 1970. Some 48 percent of the men and 43 percent of women involved had never been married. "Fundamental changes are occurring in marriage and family living" in the 1970s, the report added. It also listed several other statistics important to a consideration of American marriage and family living:

1. The divorce rate more than doubled between 1963 and 1975, to 4.8 per 1,000 population from 2.3 per 1,000. In 1976, there were 2.8 million divorced men and 4.4 million divorced women who had not married again.

2. Young adults, the report said, are waiting longer to marry. The average age at which men and women first marry increased by about one year between 1960 and 1976. Men now average 23.8 years at first marriage, while the average bride is 21.3. That figure has risen gradually, reflecting "the increasing proportion of women who exer-

cise options to advance their education and to gain employment prior to marriage."

3. Half of the 7.5 million female "heads of household" were either divorced or separated, compared with 39 percent in 1970.

In an article entitled "All Our Children, The American Family Under Pressure," a report by the Carnegie Council on Children, there are other striking statistics which shed additional light upon the modern family predicament. There has been a 700 percent increase in the number of children affected by divorce since the turn of the century. Now 54 percent of married women with school-age children work outside the home, versus only 26 percent in 1948. By the age of 16, the average child will have watched TV for more hours than he spends in school or with his parents.[6] The Carnegie Council has spent five years probing "what American society is doing to and for children." Such an inquiry is worthy of further attention.

The National Center on Child Abuse and Neglect estimates that the reported abuse cases represent only half of the child abuse that goes on. By the center's calculations, between 100,000 and 200,000 youngsters are regularly assaulted by their parents with cords, sticks, fists, hot irons, cigarettes, and booted feet. Nearly as many are sexually molested, and 700,000 are denied the food, clothing, or shelter necessary for their welfare. Every year at least 2,000 children die of abuse or neglect. "If you had a disease that affected so many children annually," says NCCAN Director Douglas Besharov, "you would call it an epidemic." Richard Gelles and two colleagues published a study of "Violence in the American Family," based on 2,143 case histories, in which they conclude that about 1 out of 33 children runs the risk of abuse or neglect.[7]

These shocking statistics and others to follow seem to substantiate the statement by G. K. Chesterton written more than 65 years ago: "If we wish to preserve the family, we must revolutionize the nation."

THE SEXUAL REVOLUTION

It is obvious that the nation has been revolutionized in the years following Chesterton's warning, but we might well question the kind of revolution that has occurred, for it has done nothing to strengthen the family. Something quite the opposite has taken place.

In 1956, Pitirim Sorokin, a prominent sociologist, reminded the nation of a fact that has recently become fully realized. He said then, "A peculiar revolution has been taking place in the lives of millions of American men and women."[8]

The sex revolution to which he referred had no revolutionary army to fight its battles. No charismatic leader championed its cause. No public relations firm organized and promoted it. It has unnoticeably proliferated because individuals acting on their own and independently of others became committed to its principles. It was never granted the appropriate press that other revolutions have received; yet it has dramatically changed the lives of men and women more than any other revolution of our time. This revolution has drastically influenced the lives of millions, deeply disturbed communities, and decisively affected the future of society.

Vance Packard seems less inclined to call the rapid change in sexual behavior a revolution because of its chaotic and varied character. Since a revolution implies a clear movement in an understood and generally supported direction, Packard terms the modern upheaval in sexual behavior, "The Sexual Wilderness."[9] Society has embarked upon an unpredictable "wilderness wandering." He reminds us that "in the past there have almost always been rules, standards, and sharply defined roles for each sex within which their maneuverings took place. Today the rules, standards, and assigned roles are in disarray."[10]

The emphasis upon sex freedom led Dr. Sorokin to warn some years ago that our sexual freedom is beginning to expand beyond the limits of safety, and is rapidly degenerating into anarchy. Sociologists would argue that the bewilderment and normlessness of the sexual revolution are in large part caused by a sense of dislocation in life produced by rapid social change.

PROLIFERATING PROMISCUITY

An increase of divorce, desertion, and the shrinking size of the family means an increase also of sexual promiscuity among more and more men and women.[11] When rules and standards are thrown out and each member of society is left to do whatever seems "right in his own eyes" (Judg. 21:25), is it any wonder that many who quite seriously would like to live moral lives, find themselves having to improvise? Anthropologist Margaret Mead compares today's lovers to two ballet dancers with no traditional lines to follow who must improvise, each wondering what the next steps will be. So many young people seem to stumble into their attitudes toward sexuality for want of a moral code. Historian Max Lerner comments, "We are living in a moral interregnum. The king is dead, but there is no king to replace him. The old standards are gone, but there are not yet new standards to take their place."[12]

We have arrived at what Sorokin said in the 1950s was "the sexualization of American culture." He noted then "that every phase of our culture had been invaded by sex." With such an assessment of that decade, one must wonder what his appraisal would be of the 1970s. "Our civilization has become so preoccupied with sex that it now oozes from all pores of American life."[13] Literature, painting and sculpture, music, stage, movies, television and radio, the popular press, advertising, even the sciences, ethics and religion, law, political life all have been affected with a kind of sex obsession.

SEX ADDICTION

Every phase of modern life is bombarded with sexual stimuli. Turn on the television, follow the cinema and consider the increased exposure of people to explicit depictions of sexual play. By the age of what was once "sweet 16" the average U.S. girl has seen depicted on motion picture or television screens several hundred demonstrations of how erotically aroused males and females embrace. Music and dancing has become more explicit and suggestive. To fast, loud, and sensual rock music, men and women perform modulated bumps and grinds before each other. To slow music, partners frequently wrap both arms around each other in snug pelvis-to-pelvis fit, swaying to and fro in a public simulation with sexual overtones. At one point "pajama dances" became popular at fraternity and sorority dances where mattresses were actually placed at the perimeter of the dance floor so that between songs couples could roll and caress if they desired.

The heavy erotic content of published materials is but another indication of American sex addiction. Pornography has become epidemic, and law enforcement officers and the courts win only an occasional battle against the floodtide of filth. Add to this the new advances being made in unveiling the female body for public display, the promotion of the dissolute look, pressures to be precocious in attracting the other sex, along with new vogues in adventure, and is it any wonder that moral underpinnings are in a state of disarray? Sorokin says, "Increasing divorce and desertion and the growth of prenuptial and extramarital sex relations are signs of sex addiction somewhat similar to drug addiction."[14] This growing sex addiction is obviously having a disastrous influence upon family life. It is utterly disruptive of family health and effects a poisoning influence upon all that is holy and good and godly. In fact, "the poison of the transgressor radiates throughout the family, then society as a whole. Social institutions are demoralized, cultural values degraded, and sex anarchy brought even closer."[15]

THE FUN MORALITY

The modern day exponents of this absurdity believe that "sex should be seen as fun, and the more sex fun a person has, the sounder he will be psychologically." Such groups as the Institute for Rational Living, with their most conspicuous spokesman, Albert Ellis, have said, "Premarital intercourse should be freely permitted and even at times encouraged for well-informed, reasonably well-adjusted persons."[16] They further recommend that "healthy adultery" (absolutely forbidden in God's Word) can help some marriages. Efforts to preserve chastity until marriage (the biblical mandate) is termed an "overt display of errant masochism." Ellis labels those as "sex fascists" who believe that certain values, in terms of which human behavior is guided, are superior.[17]

The fun morality has given way to the concept of "the fun marriage" in which partners are solely preoccupied with having a good time, parties, excursions, outings, etc., in search of the glamourous Good Life. It is totally hedonistic in outlook and operation. The effect upon the family is predictable.

RAPID SOCIAL CHANGE

The above mentioned changes have occurred in the

realm of moral revolution with profound effect upon the family. There are other changes which have played an important part in the modern family predicament. The first two I would mention perhaps have their origin in the sexual revolution.

REVERSAL OF SEXUAL ROLES

With a rising incidence of homosexuality, and the quite avant-garde concept of unisex reflected in look-alike clothing, act-alike actions, and be-alike beings, there has been considerable confusion about male and female roles. This confusion spills over into marriage. A Purdue University professor has pointed out that marriage roles that were formerly assigned by society now must be worked out by the persons involved. Newly married husbands and wives usually face a period of adjustment in which maneuverings for role advantage or clarification takes place, thus creating role tensions and conflicts.[18]

The change that has occurred in what it means to be a man and what it means to be a woman has influenced family relationships. The emphasis now is upon personhood rather than upon traditional roles for men and women.

TEMPORARY MARRIAGE

Alvin Toffler, internationally famous for his bestseller, *Future Shock*, thinks that the changes we are seeing in our families and social lives are only a symptom of things to come. He quotes Nelson Foote who said, "To expect a marriage to last indefinitely under modern conditions is to expect a lot."[19] Toffler cites the statistical odds against love as reason for the high divorce and separation rates in most of the techno-societies. "The faster the rate of change and the longer the life span, the worse these odds grow." "Something has to crack," he says, and "in point of fact . . . has already cracked."

What has cracked is the old insistence upon permanence. A conventional marriage proves itself less capable of coming through on its promise of "till death us do part." Toffler says that the idea of temporary marriage, by which he means a relationship entered into until the paths of husband and wife diverge, or when too great a discrepancy in their "developmental stages" exists, will become accepted by society. Couples will more readily call it quits without shock or embarrassment.

Toffler admits that, while some of the pain of divorce will be lessened, when the opportunity presents itself, divorced persons will marry again . . . again . . . and again. At this point temporary marriage gives way to serial marriage which is a pattern of successive temporary marriages ushering in the "Age of Transience." We have arrived.

LIFE-MODIFYING SCIENCES

One reason why temporary marriage, according to Alvin Toffler, will become widely prevalent is the fact that the average life expectancy is rising, "thereby lengthening the term during which this acrobatic feat of matched development is supposed to be maintained." Life-modifying sciences have lengthened our life span, thereby increasing the number of years a "death do us part" partnership must survive. In the 20 years between 1940 and 1960, for example, males increased their life span by 5½ years and women by 7½ years.

One other life-modifying science that has brought unprecedented change is that of birth control. Removal of the risks involved in premarital and extramarital sex together with the scientific ability to control family size have profoundly affected family life.

Technological Explosion

This is the age of technological primacy, which has created worldwide change. It is an information explosion. Dr. Mortimer Adler has stated that the available information now doubles every 8½ years.[20] This modern technological boom has brought phenomenal change and provides the motor for continual social change to which all must adapt. For example, 95 percent of all scientists who ever lived are alive and working today, and 25 percent of all the people who ever lived are alive today.[21]

High Mobility

More and more families are on the move today. Pulling up roots and changing addresses more often has created new problems for the family. A best-seller on the white collar class compares these conditions to the nursery that advertised, "We move our trees every year so they won't grow deep roots." The nursery deliberately kept the root systems on its trees shallow so they could be transplanted easily. What they failed to do is to warn that such trees, without deep roots, are not able to withstand the storm. This impermanence has created a lack of security and a growing sense of anonymity.

Eli Ginzberg, a specialist in manpower mobility at Columbia University, has suggested that America will soon be predominantly "metropolitan-type people" with few ties or commitments to longtime friends and neighbors.[22] The *Wall Street Journal* carried a report of "corporate gypsies" and cited the case of a manager of Montgomery Ward who, with his wife, had moved 28 times during their 26 years of marriage. Atlas Van Lines estimates that the average corporate manager in engineering or marketing moves about every 2½ years. Overall, the average family in the U.S. now moves 14 times in a lifetime.[23]

High mobility in our society has produced what sociologists now call "the nuclear family." Our highly industrialized society has made necessary this highly adaptable family unit, with few close kinship ties. Vance Packard defines the nuclear family as one "stripped down to parents and kids, with no grandparents, uncles, cousins, or in-laws in the living area." A whole new type of family came into existence in response to our highly industrialized age. Alvin Toffler says in *Future Shock* that "a new type of family with artificial extended kin is being formed before our very eyes." The nuclear family became the most convenient social unit for working in factories and was also better suited for moving around as the need arose in different areas, which the industrial age required. Toffler adds, "The current generation is seeing the breakdown of that factory-industrial age, as the majority of American workers have shifted from making goods in factories to providing services." The nuclear family, then, has now embarked upon a journey into the unknown.

High mobility has one other interesting sidelight. It is now easier for people to change jobs and careers. In fact, recent statistics state that the average American man changes careers three times. Not just jobs—careers. Such mobility requires flexibility. A person working with modern technology is obsolete in five years unless he participates in some sort of continuing education process.[24]

Urbanization

For years now people have been moving from the farm to the city. In 1850, 65 percent of the American people were farmers with a relatively simple life-style. In 1960, the figure was only 14 percent. Urban areas have mushroomed, creating all kinds of people problems. The home itself, in the process, has shifted from being a production center to being a self-service-station-type operation. Modern electrical conveniences along with an increased array of goods and services to make homemaking less time consuming have produced profound changes in the lifestyle of homemakers.

WORKING WOMEN

Women today represent at least 43 percent of the nation's labor force. Robert O. Blood, Jr., sociologist at the University of Michigan, believes that the increase in the number of married women—and mothers in particular—who work outside the home "is one of the most startling social changes in American History."[25] Several factors inherent in this social change affect the family. For one thing, the increase in working wives has created a new situation where many do not feel stuck because of economic necessity. Second, increased exposure to new acquaintances by working wives in a culture that gives the implied permission to try out one's attractive powers has hindered family life. Add to these an increase in social drinking by married women, and the solubility of conscience which occurs when alcohol is consumed, and it is not difficult to see that the way people live and think has been deeply affected by rapid social change. How we face social change will determine the future of the family.

THE FUTURE OF THE FAMILY

When one considers the family amidst the moral crises of our times, and the pressures both within and without, compounding every issue, it is difficult not to be pessimistic about its future. Adlai Stevenson in his final speech said, "The Family of Man, traveling together on the spaceship Earth, has a limited supply of air, water, and soil. We are preserved from annihilation only by the care

... we give our fragile craft."[26] The future of the family might well depend upon the care we give it amidst turbulent times.

Not everyone is as pessimistic about the future of the family as the statistics and conclusions might warrant. Betty Yoburg, in *The Changing Family*, writes,

> In times of severe societal crisis, the moral deterioration of the family is commonly lamented and the demise of the family is a favorite prediction of sages and seers. The present era, in America, is a fruitful one for this kind of criticism and speculation.[27]

While many raise the question of the continued necessity and desirability of a nuclear family, Ms. Yoburg insists that

> the nuclear family will not only persist into the 21st century, but it will be stronger than ever. Family as an institution will not be abolished because people expect more of it and are more apt to express and act on their dissatisfactions.[28]

"While the family is changing," says the Carnegie Council on Children, "it is not—as many sociologists fear—collapsing. Parenthood is still deeply rewarding, and more than 98 percent of all children in the U.S. still live with one or both of their parents."[29] This is good news, particularly when family life is taking on some horrendous forms—homosexual marriages, group marriages, single-parent households, and communes, to mention but a few. While these may become more prevalent along with the increased permissiveness of individual choice, "ultimately for biological reasons, and more immediately for psychological reasons," reminds Betty Yoburg, "the pairing husband and wife relationship and the exclusive parent-child relationship will endure."[30]

Our care of the family should perhaps take the form of "The Intentional Family," as suggested by Jo Carr and Imogene Sorley. Since the family finds itself in the midst of unprecedented and almost universal revolution, the rule book having been thrown away, it is no wonder people are confused. No wonder so many find themselves floundering in uncertainty. As the coauthors of *The Intentional Family* stress, "It is ours to decide whether or not we shall be a part of this upheaval that has tumbled in upon us." They continue,

> The choices we do have are whether we as a family shall try to ignore change, drag our feet and protest it, or pick up our destiny and help shape the future. The first choice is unreal; the second is its own damnation; the third is the intentional family's only available option.[31]

Although there are many forces at work against a stable home, it is still possible, like Noah, to find grace in the eyes of the Lord and strength to move out into the world with a sense of purpose and destiny. After all, the family was God's idea in the first place. Its existence is for biological, psychological, sociological, and spiritual reasons. While we cope with unprecedented change, let us determine to raise a family for God.

The enemies of the home must be identified and fitted into a Christian value system. The Bible must ever be the Source of guidance for the Christian family. The Christian family is alive and well when it follows God's rules and refuses to be "conformed to this world." While society has thrown away its rule book, the Christian reads his every day and builds those principles of morality found therein into the lives of every family member. The world needs to know that Christ is the hope of solving the modern family predicament. When families are united "in Christ," there is every chance of success, even as Noah, in days of gross wickedness. The Christian family is not a fragile craft. God has built it and it will survive so long as

Christ is honored and it intentionally guards against the pressures pitted against it.

The modern family is experiencing a locust year of devastating proportions. God has promised restoration. That process must begin with a firm foundational trust in God's basic plan for the family which included one man and one woman functioning in their respective roles, bound faithfully to one another for as long as they both live. The time has come for the Christian family to affirm its faith in the permanence of marriage as a part of God's original plan for the human race. Sexual purity must be carefully maintained, as God intended. As problems arise, creating stress and strain within the marriage and family, couples must refuse to regard divorce as a panacea for all marriage ills. Society has removed the stigma of divorce, but God's Word declares, "What ... God hath joined together, let not man put asunder" (Matt. 19:6). The future of the family under God is good. Under anything else it is a journey into the heart of the sun.

/6

LOCUSTS IN THE CHURCH

The winds of the Spirit are blowing with hurricane force in many areas of the Church today. Regardless of one's theological persuasion, it must be admitted that the coming of the neo-Pentecostal movement has produced a heightened interest in the Holy Spirit. The extraordinary, worldwide growth of the movement has, however, been viewed with mixed reactions. In some quarters of the Church it has been hailed as the greatest awakening since Pentecost and a welcome breath of fresh air in the midst of a dead formalism. As Canon Michael P. Hamilton says:

> Through enthusiastic evangelism, the movement has found support not only in local congregations, but also on university campuses, in newly founded residential communities, and in various types of societies. Those involved include laity of all professions and trades who come from a variety of economic and

educational levels. Clergy are also members, and in their number can be found bishops and ministers as well as newly ordained seminarians.[1]

An Unfortunate Atmosphere

While these individual adherents receive with enthusiasm the new hybrid Pentecostalism, others are less than enthusiastic about it. The result has been a climate of confusion and fear. Some who have not received any extraordinary spiritual "gifts" have fallen victim to a kind of spiritual inferiority complex. Because one has not received a gift such as tongues-speaking, interpretation of tongues, prophecy, or special healing powers, he is prone to think that an experience of "ordinary" faith in God is invalid. At the same time, there are those who do not consider these things necessary or even advantageous to their religious lives, and so an unfortunate atmosphere of hostility and suspicion has arisen. Many sincere believers, caught in the crossfire, are fearful, doubting, and very confused. Satan has successfully capitalized on this division of enthusiasm on the one hand and resistance on the other, to create a great polarization within the Body of Christ.

While it is a source of encouragement that the Holy Spirit is now receiving the recognition and place of prominence He has always deserved in this His dispensation, one cannot help but view our day as something of an enigma. How is it that what is welcomed by many sincere believers is at the same time dreaded and feared by other Christians who are just as devoted and sincere? It is equally puzzling that though both take the Bible seriously they come to somewhat different conclusions in their study of its meaning. It is a case of being both happy and sad at one and the same time.

The power of Satan to produce this polarization within the Body of Christ can be understood only as a locust year for the Church. Like it or not, Satan has pulled off something which will serve only to hinder Christ's cause. With all the confusion, division, and strife, Satan is enjoying victory and laughing all the way to hell that he has put one over on the Church. If Satan can continually stir up bitterness, strife, resentment, suspicion, and even outright hatred, he has successfully created the same condition as when the locusts come and destroy everything.

Many congregations have been bombarded with ardent charismatic evangelism that has caused otherwise harmonious churches to fall into division and strife. That is because of the inner compunction of the charismatics to share their "baptism in the Holy Spirit." As John Sherrill says, "The aftermath is to be propelled forward ... seeking opportunity to share the thing that has come to us."[2]

In some cases, ministers who sided with the neo-Pentecostal movement theologically have been expelled from their denominations. Churches whose denominational beliefs were contrary to that of the neo-Pentecostals have witnessed church splits with all the accompanying frustration and loss. Some church leaders who have tried to remain neutral found it impossible to be fence riders for long and have had to take firm and sometimes unpopular stands on the issue. Worse yet, homes have been shattered because one partner did, while the other did not, believe in this "new" experience.

The division cannot be viewed as a welcome event, for its thunderings have been far-reaching. It has separated denominations from denominations, churches from churches, homes from homes, individuals from individuals, even husbands from wives. The issue seems to produce an almost automatic polarization, in spite of the fact that we believe that all born-again believers are heading for the same glorious heaven, serving the same triumphant Savior, believing the same inspired Book, acknowledging the same Holy Spirit.

UNDERSTANDING DIFFERENCES

The issues seem crucial. The neo-Pentecostal shares some similarities with the older Pentecostal movement, which had already experienced the separation which comes with uniqueness. Both the old and the new mourned the loss of spiritual vitality in the Church and introduced the "baptism in the Holy Spirit" idea as the means to new life. This Spirit baptism, they both agree, is confirmed by such extraordinary evidences as speaking in tongues, healing, and exorcisms.[3] Members of the Pentecostal movement, old and new, see their emphasis as the last hope for renewal in the Church. Without doubt it has brought new, needed life into the coldness and barrenness of formalistic churches. But for all the agreement between the two Pentecostal groups, there is considerable disparity as to how their common objectives are achieved.

The newer charismatic movement has not withdrawn from the framework of the older and numerically larger denominations, but has chosen to remain within. Those who receive these purported "spiritual gifts" are encouraged to stay within their denominations, if possible, and seek to share their new experience there. Where ardent evangelism has occurred, particularly in denominations which disagree theologically with the new charismatic experience, there has been considerable disruption and division.

The older Pentecostal movement found its greatest impact among people within a lower socioeconomic strata. The newer charismatic movement has found its greatest adherents in the middle class. Both the old and new appeal to the Word of God as their authority and especially emphasize the momentous events of the Acts of the Apostles as the normative pattern for the Church today. On the other side of both the older and newer Pentecostal movements is a segment of the Body of Christ who appeal to the same Scriptures but who come to different conclusions. The result has been further polarization.

Charismania

Critics see in the newer charismatic movement a misplaced emphasis—an emphasis which makes experience the ultimate criterion of truth. There is a tendency to begin with the experience and take it to the Scriptures for divine approval, rather than start with the Scriptures and move to experience. The popularity of such a movement has developed within a society that is looking for something more than the neatly manageable formulas of this scientific and technological age. It has found fertile ground within the new experientialism manifested in such aberrations as transcendental meditation, encounter groups, Jesus "trips," and mind-bending drugs. Not all newer charismatics should be condemned because some of their number search for reality through highly charged emotional experiences thought to be supernaturally initiated, rather than through a reliable understanding of Scripture.

G. Travers Sloyers declares that "the lust after Christian experience has become a tidal wave in certain quarters of the church. To get an experience with God, whether it is scriptural or not, is the goal of even educated ministers."[4] Newer charismatics would quickly deny such an accusation because they also consider themselves people of the Book. In fact, most charismatic Christians claim to take the Bible literally and seek to justify their interpretation of the experience of Spirit baptism on scriptural grounds. James C. Logan rightly assesses that "while their religion is highly experiential, it is held to be equally biblical."[5] Their explanation is unacceptable to those outside the movement. For while the charismatics claim with evangelical fervor that they are bringing a revival of biblical Christianity, most would question whether they are biblical enough—if at all.

The controversy centers around what appears to be a tunnel vision approach to the Scriptures, especially as it relates to the spiritual gifts. Being truly biblical involves a reckoning with the whole sweep of biblical thought, not relying on proof texts to validate real, personal experiences. Hence the conclusion by Logan and others: "The controversy with charismatic Christians is not that they are unbiblical, but that they are not biblical enough."[6]

There will always be those who question the validity of what seems to be experiential faith. For example, Donald W. Burdick has stated:

> Experience, as significant as it may be, can never in itself be the criterion of truth. The devil is a past master at manufacturing deceptive experiences. The only trustworthy standard is the Word of God. Knowledge and understanding must, therefore, never be sacrificed on the altar of experience. Just as we dare not depend on feelings as a basis for assurance of salvation, so we must not allow feelings and experience to supplant the Scriptures.[7]

At issue here is what one Catholic Pentecostal has called *charismania*. Charismania is a preoccupation or fixation with *charismata*—the gifts of the Spirit. The danger is that subjective experience can become an end in itself. Experiences can become so sought after that the quality of spiritual life is gauged by who has had the most spectacular ones. When the greater desire is for feeling rather than for faith, sincere believers can be led to a difficult conclusion: To have the Spirit is to have the experience—or vice versa.

Just how this segment of the church world got to the point of an overemphasis on subjective religious experience is difficult to assess. Some say we are reaping today what was sown by theologians of a past era who prided themselves in a critical study of the Scriptures, having spent lifetimes chewing little morsels of doubt. David K. Wachtel says, "They seemed to glorify themselves rather than Christ. A cross, a fountain filled with blood, an empty tomb, a love divine, grace unlimited, and simple faith to appropriate all this were lost in a cloudy shroud of doubt."[8]

Theological uncertainty created an atmosphere void of the miraculous. The Christian Church moved through this hazy fog with more question marks than exclamation points. A kind of spiritual apathy evolved in which people were unwilling to risk anything for the question marks. There was not enough being believed with confidence for anyone to get enthused about, much less totally involved in. So spiritual lethargy became normative in the Church. And rather than dwell on the great affirmations and certainties of faith, people began to doubt their beliefs and believe their doubts. The need for revival and renewal within the Christian Church became marked.

Denial of the supernatural and a playing down of emphasis on good, healthy emotion in religious expression created a vacuum that has been filled in many places by the modern, neo-Pentecostal movement. Who could have ever predicted that in 1906 what was happening at a meeting in an abandoned stable would spread throughout the entire church world, affecting both Protestants and Catholics alike? That meeting called for a "baptism in the Holy Spirit" which would be confirmed by the external sign of speaking in tongues. This is generally held to be the birth of the modern-day tongues movement. The reverberations of Azusa Street continue to resound.

All Spirit-filled believers share a common desire to see renewal and revival within the Body of Christ. If they do not, they certainly should. That many have received a dramatic or quiet life-energizing encounter through the charismatic movement should be cause for joy. But while the desire for a deepened devotion, a revitalized prayer life, and a renewed emphasis on the person and work of the Holy Spirit has been shared by all Christians, many sincere believers see in the emphasis upon the external signs accompanying the baptism with the Holy Spirit, an extreme swing of the pendulum that well could be termed "charismania."

When an individual's spirituality is judged solely in terms of the enthusiasm of his experiential life, there is just cause for alarm. James C. Logan states it clearly, "*Charismania* fails to appreciate the full power of God to inspire the complete person, who is rational mind and ethical will as well as feeling heart."[9] This appraisal grows out of Jesus' summary of the law in Matt. 22:37 which is the normative pattern for Christian experience: "Love the Lord your God with all your heart, with all your soul and with all your mind" (NIV).

The work of the Holy Spirit in the life of a believer deals with the whole person. From hence comes the criticism of the newer charismatics that they go on "heart trips" instead of "head trips"; that rational faculties are of lesser importance than affectional faculties. According to Jesus' words, both are involved. Neo-Pentecostalists need to be reminded that in their search for a deepened experientialism, they should avoid the danger of anti-intellectualism.

Importance of Sound Doctrine

Another area of wide disparity within Christendom deals with the matter of doctrine. Is it important or not? To be sure, not all newer charismatics share the view that doctrine is unimportant, but there are many who believe that at best it is inconsequential. It is said that what is most important is to follow the Holy Spirit wherever He leads. It is very puzzling that doctrine is relegated to a place of relative unimportance, while the Bible is cited as the basis of authority for the modern charismatic experience. When their preestablished conclusions are not reached in the process of biblical exegesis and interpretation, they seem to find it easy to bypass the doctrinal implications.

The ultimate appeal to experience occurs because of a misunderstanding of the nature of doctrine. Doctrine is the structure of our faith. Our faith takes its shape through the guidance of the Holy Spirit throughout the entire process of interpreting God's Word. Without the structural solidarity afforded by sound doctrine, it is easy to find oneself in the condition described by Paul in Eph. 4:14—"tossed back and forth by the waves, and blown here and there by every wind of teaching" (NIV). Paul uses the metaphor of a rudderless skiff adrift on the sea to describe the immaturity of some within the Body of Christ. And yet it is an apt description of those who do not know what they believe or why. In a condition like that it is perilously easy to be governed, not by the principles of sound doctrine, but by the pulsation of blazing emotions. It is equally impossible to develop right living from wrong doctrine.

Psychological Considerations

Still another aspect of the controversy is the stir over

the psychological dangers which frequently accompany the experience-centered faith of the newer charismatics. Satan is capitalizing on the opportunity to mastermind deceptive, counterfeit experiences, much to the chagrin of those who believe their experience is biblically valid. Recent psychological studies have gone a long way to remove some of the old myths that have plagued even the older Pentecostal movements. It is now generally recognized that Pentecostals are no less healthy mentally than any other Christians. No one seriously believes that to be a part of the charismatic movement means a person is in psychological trouble.

It is very difficult to assess the psychological dangers because those who claim to have received the gift of tongues thoroughly believe their experience is from God. On the other hand, many are quick to say that glossolalia is "of the devil." It is easy to make broad generalizations about things one does not understand. That is exactly what the Pharisees did when they could not understand how Jesus derived His miraculous power to cast the demons out of a blind and mute man. They said, "It is only by Beelzebub, the prince of demons, that this fellow drives out demons" (Matt. 12:24, NIV). The defense of His holy power led Jesus to make one of the sternest warnings in Scripture:

> "I tell you, every sin and blasphemy will be forgiven men, but the blasphemy against the Spirit will not be forgiven. Anyone who speaks a word against the Son of Man will be forgiven, but anyone who speaks against the Holy Spirit will not be forgiven, either in this age or in the age to come" (Matt. 12:31-32, NIV).

The unpardonable sin is to attribute the Holy Spirit's work to the work of the devil. That is not only blasphemous but unforgivable.

Many genuine Christians within the newer

charismatic movement are deeply committed to the Lord and simply want to know God as fully as possible. That is the worthy goal of every Christian, and whatever that takes they are willing to do. If that be speaking in tongues, then they are willing to seek that external accompaniment. It should not be interpreted, then, as a depreciation of their devotion. It merely points up the danger of accepting a psychological substitute in the "whatever that takes" process.

Many Christians with no less devotion and desire to know God as fully as possible question the biblical validity of an experience which is psychologically induced. The whole idea of "coaching" seekers in the art of speaking in tongues has raised some serious questions and served to widen the polarization within Christendom. Oral Roberts, in his book *The Holy Spirit in the Now I*, states that in all the years of his Pentecostal ministry where he has prayed for people to receive the gift, "in every case" where the person was open and not tense and inhibited, "everyone" received it. He believes any born-again believer can speak in tongues immediately, "if he knows how."[10]

It is the "telling how" that disturbs so many non-charismatics. One charismatic leader instructed tongues seekers at Yale University in the following way:

(1) Think visually and concretely, i.e., try to visualize Jesus as a person.
(2) Consciously yield your voice and organ of speech to the Holy Spirit.
(3) Repeat elementary sounds, e.g., Alleluia, alleluia, alleluia . . .
(4) He then laid his hands on the head of each seeker, prayed, and the seeker began to speak in tongues.[11]

It is difficult to justify the validity of inducement to speak in tongues. The explanation for such yields itself to an entirely psychological explanation. It could be simply the result of ecstasy, a condition of emotional exaltation, in which, according to George B. Cutten, "the one who experiences it is more or less oblivious of the external world, and loses to some extent his self-consciousness and his power of rational thought and self-control."[12]

Still another possible psychological explanation is that of hypnosis or autosuggestion. "In the former," says Donald W. Burdick, "a person directs his undivided attention toward some particular object, then lets his mind become blank and yields to the hypnotist's suggestions." When a person initiates these suggestions from within himself, it is autohypnosis or autosuggestion. As in the Yale University situation, the tongues seeker focuses visually and concretely on Jesus; yields his mind, tongue, and voice; then begins repeating similar sounds. The result is glossolalia.

Other possible psychological explanations exist which are beyond the scope of this book to consider in detail: namely, psychic catharsis, exalted memory, an intense desire to escape conflict, the breakthrough of the unconscious, or some other temporary psychological abnormality. There is understandable reticence for anyone to become involved in this, for the very reason that the "experience" may be explained psychologically as abnormal. Invariably, the intensity of desire on the part of the tongues seeker to experience the phenomenon has led to some unfortunate abuses, which will continue to make people wary of it.

DEMONIC COUNTERFEITS

This intensity of desire on the part of some to receive the gift of tongues at any cost or by any means has allowed Satan to disguise himself as an angel of light to the deception of many. If Satan could master a demon's counterfeit experience, many, though very sincere, would be deceived. Wesley L. Duewel reminds us that "the Bible warns that there is the possibility of demonic tongues" in 1 Cor. 12:3. Satan through his demons often "masquerades as an angel of light" (2 Cor. 11:14, NIV). This deceitful action of Satan can be in many forms, one being the counterfeiting of the ministry and gifts of the Spirit, as 2 Cor. 11:3-15 shows. Duewel expresses the concern that "demonic motivation in the area of emotion can lead to fanaticism and unwholesome frenzy." As long as the tongues experience can be counterfeited by Satan, it will remain suspect.

It is well documented that demonic tongues have been experienced in many parts of the world among the spiritist religions and in some cases found to be a part of seances and the evil world of the occult. In *The Modern Tongues Movement* Gromacki quotes a former Chinese missionary, Dr. Raymond Frame: "Evil spirits can easily find opportunity to operate in the believer's emotional life—especially when the believer is persuaded to suspend all intellectual activity and to yield his will over to an invisible intelligence."[13]

The neo-Pentecostal asserts, however, that the yielding is to the Holy Spirit. It is essential, then, to "try the spirits whether they are of God: because many false prophets are gone out into the world" (1 John 4:1). John goes on to tell how: "Hereby know ye the Spirit of God: Every spirit that confesseth that Jesus Christ is come in the flesh is of God: and every spirit that confesseth not that Jesus Christ is come in the flesh is not of God: and this is that spirit of antichrist, whereof ye have heard that it should come; and even now already is it in the world" (vv. 2-3). When a sincere believer becomes so absorbed in tongues, the least of all the gifts of the Spirit, and elevates it to a position of prominence, Dr. Frame warns, "he places himself in a particularly vulnerable position in relation to the danger of demon oppression, obsession, or actual possession."[14]

FAILURE TO COMPROMISE

For the present, it seems that the polarization will not soon be reconciled. Those who are committed to the neo-Pentecostal movement are not ready to relent in their discovery of what they consider to be a new experience of the Spirit. But neither are non-charismatics going to yield in their understanding of the Spirit's ministry to the whole person as in the Scriptures. So Satan is forcing the issue. The more chaos and confusion he can stir up, the better. The devil is the author of confusion. Satan can create total chaos when doctrinal compromise is forced upon a local church. If that happens, the locusts of doubt, division, and disillusionment will swarm in until at times it is difficult to see the light of God's truth. Whenever Old Slewfoot can achieve the division of families and churches, cause friendships to be forsaken, and help loyalties to be abandoned, he has Christians right where he wants them.

To force divisive issues on a local church or to try to impose these two opposing theologies upon each other is to play havoc in the church. As long as charismatics and non-charismatics both continue to believe their understanding is biblically correct and experientially true, the seeds of confusion and chaos will persist. And as this great polarization continues, the locust year of the church will never end.

/7

MORALS AND THE MEDIA

The locusts of immorality began swarming over the airwaves of our land almost without notice with the coming of a media which has proven to be both a blessing and a curse. New vistas of knowledge have been reached and a new level of enlightenment attained with the appearance of instant, mass communication. But with all the noticeable achievement one cannot help but believe that the locusts have begun to swarm over the moral structure of society, producing devastating flux, change, and erosion. It is nothing less than a locust year for morality, and one wonders if so powerful a medium as television has not had the greatest influence.

On February 6, 1977, Dr. Richard Palmer, president of the AMA, asked 10 major corporations to stop sponsoring violent television shows. He said, among other things,

"These shows pollute the airwaves." And from time to time others have urged the television networks to review policies which support violent programming. Dr. Palmer raised the issue by saying, "TV has been quick to raise questions of social responsibility with industries which pollute the air. In my opinion, television through its access to airwaves may be creating a more serious problem of air pollution."[1] He expresses the legitimate concern that "if the programming of a child consists largely of being exposed to violent content, then his perceptions of the real world may be significantly distorted," and ended his remarks by urging major advertisers "to recognize the medical aspects of their advertising programs and consider its impact on society."[2]

In addition to the social, medical, and psychological issues at stake, there are significant moral and religious questions which must be addressed to a media with almost unlimited access to the minds of people. Today's television finds itself in the position occupied by radio in the previous era. Television is the "mass medium" in the truest sense. Don Jamieson says, "No means of communication more properly warrants the description."[3] He noted that Canadians watch TV and listen to radio more than any other people on earth. Each week the picture tube and loudspeaker occupy their attention for more hours than most Canadians spend earning a living. When one begins to analyze what such exposure to the media of TV is doing to our world, it is here that many untested assumptions, personal experiences and convictions, and often prejudice and bias enter the discussion. No one seems confident enough to say just what this massive exposure is doing; they only admit, as Jamieson has, that "broadcasting is changing lives with results that will be far reaching for them and for their country."[4]

A Difficult Inquiry

It is a difficult assignment to try to assess the effect of television on people's lives. Perhaps this is the reason why there is so little research data available. Vincent T. Wasilewski, then president of the National Association of Broadcasters, appeared in March of 1969 before the Senate Subcommittee on Communications, Committee on Commerce, and expressed the problem accurately. He said,

> Many people are impatient that precise answers to the question of TV's effect on children are not available. The major problem is the nature of research required. The questions posed and answers sought are extremely complex. The questions we are really asking are: Why do people behave as they do? What are the root causes of human behavior? This is probably the most difficult area in all research in which to produce reliable information.[5]

Although it is a difficult inquiry, it is admitted, however, that television has a profound effect. For example, William H. Stewart, M.D., the surgeon general in 1969, said, "There is little doubt that television and television violence have an impact on the viewing public—adults as well as children. The still unanswered question is, 'What kind of impact and how does it influence behavior?' "[6]

There is an effect, but it is difficult to identify. Perhaps it is a case of allowing this new technology to catch us unprepared. What makes the consequences more frightening is to study the length of exposure to broadcasting's impact. By the age of 16, the average American child has spent more hours in front of a TV than in the classroom. Recent statistics indicate that between the ages of 3 and 18 the average American spends 22,000 hours watching TV. David Seamands says, "That same average American, if he is a better than average church goer, only spends 3,000 hours in Sunday School and church-related activities."[7]

TV's Impact on National Character

It is clear that our "oral and aural" culture can exert influence over the marketplace of ideas. The world of sight and sound is having an impact on national character which, according to one psychiatrist's estimate, is "fraught with new dimensions of habit-forming and conditioning behavior, to say nothing of the power of suggestion, which by repetition can also become hypnotic."[8]

William Elliott reminds us that television is a child of the American culture, a child so lusty and with powers so formidable that it may assume a more and more dominant role in forming the basic nature of American habits, just as the combustion engine, within little more than a half century, transformed a civilization out of all recognition. Television, within little more than a decade of its actual use by the public, has penetrated every quarter of America.[9] When George Orwell wrote his book *1984*, he envisioned a society dominated with conformity and fear and symbolized by ever-present television screens controlled by "Big Brother." The vision is only partly prophetic because, as William P. Dizard says, "We probably have the wit and the will to avoid the political tyranny Orwell described." But he is right to caution that "we may be less skillful in coping with the brash, ubiquitous power of television."[10]

Well before 1984, television became the world's most influential mass communications media. On Super Bowl XI Sunday an estimated 75 million people around the world watched the Oakland Raiders beat the Minnesota Vikings. Super Bowl XII reached an estimated audience of 95 million. Television stations in over 90 countries today serve an audience of over 750 million persons. TV's influence, according to Dizard, will stretch "from Minsk to Manila, from London to Lima, and on to the Nigerian up-country city of Kaduna where even now bearded camel drivers and local tribesmen sit in fascinated harmony before a teahouse television set watching Bonanza."[11]

Television has reached a place of prominence in the world very quickly and with such far-reaching influence that our technological age has not time to define its purpose nor set its goals. We can be sure only that television is here, and that whatever the implications, television will soon be the first medium to be shared and understood by virtually everyone on earth.

Never was a single emotion shared by so many people as on the day in November, 1963, when 300 million persons on four continents watched the televised funeral of a murdered American president. Television is not only a recorder of events in a revolutionary age; it is, by its persuasive immediacy, a major tool for shaping the age.[12] In 1977, NBC ran a "Segment 3" inquiry on Journalistic Diplomacy. The point was emphasized that broadcast journalists were either reporting events or serving to help shape peace initiatives in the Middle East. No one seemed certain enough to say which was the case. Dizard is again right in his summary of TV:

> Presenting with electronic impartiality not only reality but also the fantasies which cushion us from reality, it is the ultimate instrument of both confrontation and escape. Television serves this double function with a subtlety that makes it the despair of those who try to define its purposes.[13]

Adverse Effects

The time has come to begin asking some serious questions about the adverse effect of this mass medium upon the minds and hearts of people. One recurrent note in most discussions of this type is that so little is definitely known or can be proved concerning the harmful effects of television. A trip to a good library to research the subject of television's effect on society only ends in frustration over the scarcity of knowledge. Harry J. Skornia has written one of the few books on the subject, and he reminds us that "every new technology catches its age unprepared."[14] This is exactly what TV has done to the viewing public. It has caught them off guard. When you begin to analyze the type of material that parades itself before the public eye, there is no question of influence; the real issue is what may be done about it. Skornia says, "Radio and television not only can and do teach, but they cannot help but teach. There is no longer any question of whether they teach. It is only a question of what they teach, whether intentionally or unintentionally."[15]

Of all the places where the so-called new morality has deadened our moral sensitivity and undermined the biblical basis of our beliefs, television has had the most profound effect. It has happened with little resistance. Psychiatrists have repeatedly warned that nothing affects people as much as what they do not take seriously. Harry Skornia relates that there is substantial evidence that people often hypnotically watch whatever is offered. The media is all-engulfing. It involves the whole person kinesthetically, subliminally, emotionally, as well as intellectually. There is no escaping the influence of the broadcasting media, according to Skornia, "for what does not reach the individual directly from it, reaches him indirectly through his peers and reference groups."[16]

Conflicting Values

The Christian has a right to ask what effect is being exerted by the electronic knowledge industry over the marketplace of ideas. In the area of values it must be acknowledged that those responsible for television are predominately materialistic. Anything that does not fit this pattern is shunned. The Christian is repeatedly called upon to reconcile the conflict between the value system taught by the Bible, the church, the (traditional) school, and the laws of society with those taught by the mass media. When strain can no longer be tolerated, something has to give. This has led seriously concerned people to comment, "Is it any wonder that conflicting value systems and the need to reconcile them has created an increased national incidence of schizophrenia?" Dizard says,

> The demands made on children to reconcile conflicting values, to adjust back and forth many times a day between values taught by television fantasy and the values that the reality of his personal life requires of him constitute strains that not all are capable of meeting. Mental hospitals and prisons are full of people who could not make such adjustments.[17]

Plato had a premise that is apropos today: "The mind grows by what it feeds on." Albert Einstein, recognizing certain character attributes in life, said, "It is essential that the student acquire an understanding and a lively feeling for value. He should acquire a vivid sense of the beautiful and the morally good. Otherwise, he with his specialized knowledge more closely resembles a well-trained dog than a harmoniously developed individual."

If value is that important, how does one reconcile conflicting values with which he is continually bombarded? Infidelity is glamorized in a variety of ways: in emotion-manipulating melodrama; in cleverly wrapped puns; on talk shows, proud of their candor, the idea of promiscuous sex is promoted. Off-color humor, use of God's name in vain, promiscuous behavior are all presented as normative behavior. As David A. Seamands says, "What is most indicative are the subtle ways in which the basic standards of marital fidelity are ridiculed or openly mocked."[18]

Almost without the slightest resistance, people have yawned their way through the undercutting of moral fibre which is the strength of any nation, home, or individual.

An all-out war has been waged on traditional Judeo-Christian values. Once, four-letter words were bleeped from the tapes of the televised media. Now, because of a gradual onslaught, words like *hell* and *damn* freely flow from the lips of television personalities, whom tragically so many tend to worship as heroes. But it is not just the new freedom to use improper words that bothers concerned people as much as the type of sexual mores that have come to be socially acceptable. Premarital and extramarital sex are condoned if not openly encouraged. Now other forms of heretofore condemned sexual behavior, namely, homosexuality and lesbianism, have had the stigma removed. The sad thing is that the war has only begun. Christian groups like the Committee Against Blasphemy on Television have begun to organize Christians in an effort to fight back and say, "We have had it with the erosion of our morality!" One wonders, though, if the tide can be turned.

It is surprising that most Christians have been docile to the locusts of immorality that have swarmed the airwaves. If you take a frog and place him in a pail of boiling water, he will immediately jump out. But if you place him in a pail of cold water and heat it gradually, the frog will stay there and be boiled to death. This is essentially what has happened in the area of moral values. A sure, steady war has been waged through a medium people supposedly do not take seriously, and all at once we find ourselves morally insensitive.

Many have begun to register alarm over the effect of TV violence upon the minds of people, particularly children. Mayor Palmer Gaillard of Charleston, S.C., spoke out against crime-and-violence television programs in his address to the NAACP's Summit Conference on Crime held in his city. He said, "It's high time we said we don't want this sort of thing here any longer."[19] People who wrote letters of comment to the local newspaper said things like,

> Movies and television are riddled with an oversupply of sex and violence and it has had a profound effect upon all elements of our society. TV has had an eroding effect on morals in our country. It has encouraged lawlessness and given impetus to our rising crime rate. Anyone with any degree of intelligence would realize that this is so and more and more people must speak out against this maddening situation.[20]

The television industry is not willing to admit the validity of such criticism. They cite in defense of the media that television is a strong influence against crime, rather than a cause. Bad people always lose on TV-adventure programs. TV crime and violence cannot be blamed for all real-life violence. One newspaper editor showed the greater wisdom when he said,

> TV crime can't be blamed for all real-life violence. The problem runs much, much deeper than that. However, it can be blamed for providing for impressionable young minds a blueprint, a pattern, for aggressive behavior. Just as language and habits are learned through constant exposure, it isn't unreasonable to think that resort to violence to resolve conflict can be learned through the constant viewing of these type of programs.[21]

If that is true concerning violent, aggressive behavior, is it not also true of moral values? It is interesting that recently Mexico forbade the showing of some American TV programs in their country. The simple reason given was that the shows did not have anything to do with building character value and could only lead to inciting poverty-stricken people to violence.

An article appeared in *U.S. News and World Report* on

January 13, 1975, entitled "TV Sex and Violence—Showdown Nears Washington." It was reported that a new wave of complaints about the fare being offered on home screens is prompting this warning to television's rulers: "Clean up or else!" The public and even officials in Washington frequently apply pressure to the television industry. The above article made it clear that increasing portrayals of violence and sex on TV despite past promises of TV executives to change their ways, was the cause of much of the trouble.

The trouble is that most of the promises made have been broken. More and more programs requiring viewer discretion have hit the airwaves. And what is viewer discretion anyway? Particularly is this a problem when Mother and Dad work and many children are left home alone, or when many parents couldn't care less what their children watch.

The controversy continues along with the outcry. While everyone waits for something to be done, nothing gets done, and the gradual erosion of morality and values continues at an alarming rate. Because no one knows what to do, they do nothing. When the public outcry gets loud enough, Congress and the FCC schedules another hearing, but any change is always short-lived. One group of concerned Christians lead by Pastor Donald E. Wildmon of Southaven, Miss., enlisted more than 1,000 churches to turn off their sets for a week to protest "the pervasive violence and cheapened sex on television."[22] Rev. Wildmon rightly declared the sentiments of many concerned Christians when he said, "For years concerned citizens have pleaded in vain with the networks to stop the deterioration in programming that is corroding the mental and moral climate of our society."[23]

With sinister subtlety the locusts came eating away at our moral sensitivity. It was not sudden but gradual.

Premarital sex used to be frowned upon even in a godless society. Now it is openly encouraged. Whereas the decisions among young people used to be whether to kiss on the first date, now the decision is whether to have sexual intercourse on the first date. Adultery is now presented as the norm in marital experience. And the by-product? One out of every two marriages ends in divorce. Though not overnight, this erosion of morality happened just the same. A generation ago if a girl became pregnant out of wedlock, she was shunned by society and would usually have to go away with her husband to make a new life where they were unknown. Not anymore. It happens now so frequently both within and without the churches that it has lost its social stigma.

There is cause for alarm when the number of unwanted pregnancies among teenage girls throughout the nation has reached epidemic proportions, according to family planning experts. They are now saying that along with drugs and venereal disease, pregnancy has become one of the most serious health problems among teenagers. To deal with the problem of unwanted pregnancy, various methods of birth control were offered through federally funded agencies such as Planned Parenthood. The Supreme Court recently upheld the ruling that parental permission was unnecessary to receive such help. And since, according to the Planned Parenthood representative, "no 100% effective birth control method other than total abstinence exists,"[24] is it any wonder that abortion in our country has become the viable option for vast numbers of women?

It is not enough that the broadcast media know, or should know, the impact of their programs upon children, nor that they know about the marketing of emotions and of the prurient interest in violence and sex their fare excites. It is time the television industry starts to consider the greater purposes that television should serve. While total blame for all of society's evil cannot be laid at the feet of the television industry, to admit that it has been a contributing factor in the moral erosion of our times is no overstatement.

The locusts came swarming over our morality and the results have been devastating. To cope with the change, the idea of a "new morality" was invented. But Christians everywhere recognized that for what it was: simply the old immorality brought up to date. The Christian community will need to continue its outcry along with concerned moral citizens. And if the media will not listen, the buck must stop with people who must, in the interest of protecting proper moral tone, exercise their prerogative to censor what comes into their homes and minds, by turning "the boob tube" off.

Parental guidance is strongly suggested for parents as well as children. Children must be protected from the distorted value system of this godless age. An educated Christian conscience that is sensitive to what is morally right must be active in the process of personal censorship. If we allow ourselves and our children to soak in a conflicting moral value system, there will not only be very severe strain but also the added result of moral and spiritual desensitivity. If that point is reached, no one will care enough to fight for right anymore. Morality will be a thing of the past, forgotten, dead, and gone.

/8

ALL THEM ALL THINGS

I grew up in the days when the television western made really good entertainment. There was Hopalong Cassidy, Roy Rogers, Sky King, even the Lone Ranger and Tonto. One unique characteristic of each western was the good guys and bad guys. The good guys always wore the white hats, while the bad guys wore the black hats. You could pretty well tell what kind of person he was by the color of his hat. The bad guys would always be robbing banks, rustling cattle, or kidnapping the sheep rancher's daughter. The hero would catch the villain, free the hostages, and always fall in love, in the process, with the rancher's daughter. They would be married and the final scene would be that heroic couple riding off into the sunset to live happily ever after.

It was good entertainment before the day of crude

realism forced its way upon us. Somewhere along the line we began to focus upon what we already knew deep inside. And that is that life does not roll along in storybook style with everyone living happily ever after. Very few Christians seem to move through this world on an ever ascending scale, free from worry and woe. There are some, however, who enjoy good health, happiness, success, a happy homelife, a serene old age, and finally a glorious exit to heaven. Even if there are only a few like that, something within everyone wants to rejoice with those whose lives have been so blessed.

But for the great majority of people, life just doesn't follow the storybook pattern. In fact, much of the time it is just the opposite. There are disappointments, broken dreams, sorrow and suffering, and seemingly endless situations which cause us to be perplexed. We try to understand but it just doesn't make sense. If it were confined to those who do not love God and it came as a result of their sin, it might be easier to understand, but it is not. The Christian is no more immune from tragedy and heartache than anyone else. There is the real enigma. He is pressed to ask, "Why?" Not only "Why them?" but "Why me, Lord, what have I ever done?"

Job's Predicament

Job faced that same dilemma when he knew deep within himself that there was no sin in his life, that he had served God and tried to do right all along, but here he was reduced to a pitiful mass of running sores, able only to sit by the fire and scratch himself while his accusers came to "comfort" him. They said, "Job, the problem is that there is sin in your life!" "God always punishes sinners." "Job, you're getting what you deserve." "Now what was it you did to grieve God in this way?" The Book of Job is filled with about 30 chapters where three men try to comfort Job in his misery. But all their pious moralizing only served to drive Job into deeper despair. After a fourth man, younger than the rest, sought to refocus Job's vision, God finally spoke to Job from the whirlwind to say, "Stand up like a man and brace yourself for battle" (40:7, TLB). By the time God had finished setting Job straight about His providence, the only thing left for Job was to admit,

> "I know that you can do anything and that no one can stop you. You ask who it is who has so foolishly denied your providence. It is I. I was talking about things I knew nothing about and did not understand, things far too wonderful for me" (42:2-3, TLB).

The God who had allowed Satan to test His servant, now blessed Job again. The Lord restored his wealth and happiness and gave Job twice as much as before. The Lord blessed Job at the end of his life more than at the beginning. Job was restored.

The lesson of Job is clear enough for all to understand. No amount of pious platitudes on why the righteous suffer can soothe a breaking heart. And yet good people, faithful Christian people, continue to ask, "Do you suppose God is punishing me for something I did wrong?" The question must be answered. In Job's case, Satan did the dirty work, not God. Satan tried to question the integrity of Job by saying he was only serving God for the loaves and fishes: "Take away his wealth, and you'll see him curse you" (1:11, TLB). But God knew Job better than Satan, for it did not work. When his family and houses and lands were destroyed, Job went on serving God. Then Satan said, "Touch his body with sickness and he will curse you" (2:5, TLB). Again, God knew better, and He allowed Satan to bring physical suffering to Job, but He would not let him take his life. During his fiery ordeal, Job would say, "Though he slay me, yet will I trust in him" (13:15). Job did not whistle his way through the suffering.

And he did what everyone who has ever suffered will do. He asked, "Why?" In Job's case, as in ours, Satan should have been accused, not God.

But God all too often gets blamed for the things He allows us to pass through as if He caused them. Sure, Job got angry—he was hurting—but he did not charge God foolishly or deny his faith. No Christian should give Satan that opportunity. No one has ever come up with a solution to all the dilemmas of life. Some things must be put in a category entitled "Things That Don't Make Sense."

Paul's Sufferings

Paul had a long list of them in his life. He pulls back the curtain of his life to reveal some of them in his Second Letter to the Corinthians (11:23-28, NIV).

> Are they servants of Christ? (I am out of my mind to talk like this.) I am more. I have worked much harder, been in prison more frequently, been flogged more severely, and been exposed to death again and again. Five times I received from the Jews the forty lashes minus one. Three times I was beaten with rods, once I was stoned, three times I was shipwrecked, I spent a night and a day in the open sea, I have been constantly on the move. I have been in danger from rivers, in danger from bandits, in danger from my own countrymen, in danger from Gentiles; in danger in the city, in danger in the country, in danger at sea; and in danger from false brothers. I have labored and toiled and have often gone without sleep; I have known hunger and thirst and have often gone without food; I have been cold and naked. Besides everything else, I face daily the pressure of my concern for all the churches.

Before Paul had the courage to openly discuss his sufferings he gives a glimpse of his own attitude toward the locusts in his life. In 2 Cor. 4:8-10 (NIV) he says,

> We are hard pressed on every side, but not crushed; perplexed, but not in despair; persecuted, but not abandoned; struck down, but not destroyed. We

always carry around in our body the death of Jesus, so
that the life of Jesus may also be revealed in our body.

Perplexed, but Not Despairing

There are people all over the world who are not only perplexed but in utter despair. They are not smiling their way through their difficulties, nor are they "whistling through the graveyard." They constantly encounter dilemmas that do not make sense. Much of it—well, most of it I simply do not understand. It did not make sense when my mother was taken from us at age 53. It did not make sense that my wife's mother was taken with cancer when my wife was only 7. The tragedy, pain, sorrow, and sickness, the disappointments and anguish, the broken dreams and trouble will never make sense. I have been perplexed, you have been perplexed, there will probably be more of the same to face in the future. But, somehow, because the grace of our Lord Jesus Christ is sufficient, there is blessed hope. And we are promised that "all things work together for good to them that love God, to them who are the called according to his purpose" (Rom. 8:28).

Riddles in the World

Just how God works in all things to bring about good will always remain a mystery in this life. Especially when there are things in the world that do not make sense. In the little Book of Habakkuk we find the prophet in the midst of perplexity because things were happening in his world that did not make sense. He cried out to God,

> O Lord, how long must I call for help before you will listen? I shout to you in vain; there is no answer.
> "Help! Murder!" I cry, but no one comes to save. Must I forever see this sin and sadness all around me? Wherever I look there is oppression and bribery and men who love to argue and to fight. The law is not

enforced and there is no justice given in the courts, for the wicked far outnumber the righteous, and bribes and trickery prevail (1:1-4, TLB).

A look at the world today makes one feel the same way at times. For Habakkuk, perplexity was not his final word. The Lord himself speaks and says, "Look, and be amazed! You will be astounded at what I am about to do! For I am going to do something in your own lifetime that you will have to see to believe" (v. 5, TLB). It was as if the Lord was saying "Though it may now look as though all things are stacked against you and you are perplexed; though the time that I take in balancing the scales and righting the wrongs may not be swift in coming, I will work in all these things."

PEOPLE PUZZLES

In addition to a lot of things in the world that do not make sense, there are a lot of things people do that just don't make any sense either. Have you ever wondered how Jacob fitted the sudden loss of his favorite son, Joseph, into a pattern for good? I never liked the fact that he played favorites with Joseph either. That played a large part in the way things turned out, for his brothers became so jealous of him that they decided to rid themselves of the problem. They would destroy Joseph. So they sold him into slavery in Egypt and bloodied his coat for an explanation to Jacob that he had been killed by wild animals. Jacob got so depressed about this and some subsequent events years later that one day he said, "All these things are against me" (Gen. 42:36).

As it turned out they were not, but that would only be learned sometime after that. All things cannot be against us if all things work together for good. It was the working together that really hurt. Only after a famine had struck hard and Jacob had sent his sons to buy bread in Egypt more than once was he able to see how all these things were clearly a part of God's greater plan to save Israel from famine. Even Joseph would come to say to the same brothers who wronged him, "Ye thought evil against me; but God meant it unto good" (Gen. 50:20). And through it all, God's people were spared starvation.

On the surface, difficulties and real life perplexities drive us to think that all these things are against us. The well-worn illustration of the handsewn bookmark is still speaking a truth for today. On the reverse side you see only a meaningless tangle of loose ends; but on the side where you read, "God Is Love," there is order and meaning. Just like Jacob and Joseph, life often puts us on the wrong side of God's providences, and the threads make no sense whatsoever. But to God they make sense, for He understands the end from the beginning.

Into His hands must go the things that people do that don't make sense. Imagine how John the Baptist must have felt sitting there in prison, no doubt pondering why Jesus was elsewhere working miracles, content to leave His forerunner in jail to face execution alone. Or how Paul must have felt after Demas had forsaken him, being in love with the world more than God's work. None of us have to think too long to remember a Demas or two in our lives, someone we counted on but who let us down.

When people let us down, there are no assurances that we will smile through it. There will be tears of anguish. It will hurt and certainly it will not make sense. There will be perplexity, but there need not be despair. The Christian will not give up and quit if he will place his confidence in Jesus, the Author and Finisher of his faith. He need not sever his relationship with Christ because someone fails and tragically sins. It didn't make sense to me when a good friend tragically sinned and broke up his home. It would have been easy to conclude, as some do when people they have confidence in let them down, that "there is nothing to this business of Christianity anyway!" Why abandon faith over someone else's failure?

Every minister shares a sense of loss whenever a fellow minister loses out because of some tragic moral failure in his life. That is why a Christian dare not let his relationship with Christ depend on people. People make mistakes. People hurt. People sin. People disappoint. People are human. People succumb to temptation. People believe Satan's lies. God is the One who never fails, who never disappoints, who always heals and helps and soothes and lifts, not people. The focus of our inner faith must be on the Lord of glory who alone is trustworthy and dependable. *Jesus never fails!*

It is known that Paul wrote his Second Letter to the Corinthians, among other reasons, to defend his apostleship, which had come under severe criticism. There were some who rose up in arrogant defiance of Paul both as a minister and person. Perhaps this is why he referred to a visit to Corinth as a "painful visit" (2:1, NIV). Apparently after he left, the charges and slurs against his character gained momentum. People questioned his motives, his behavior, his courage, his abilities, even his apostolic ministry, which looked like was about to be ruined.

So instead of going personally and putting the people and himself through a painful ordeal, he wrote his second letter. Do his words reveal a man who is disappointed? Defeated? In despair over his critics? No, not at all. Instead he said,

> I call upon this God to witness against me if I am not telling the absolute truth: the reason I haven't come to visit you yet is that I don't want to sadden you with a severe rebuke. When I come, although I can't do much to help your faith, for it is strong already, I want

> to be able to do something about your joy: I want to
> make you happy, not sad (1:23-24, TLB).

And what about the church member whose scandalous conduct caused Paul so much heartache? His magnanimous reply came through clearly:

> Remember that the man I wrote about, who caused all the trouble, has not caused sorrow to me as much as to all the rest of you—though I certainly have my share in it too. I don't want to be harder on him than I should. He has been punished enough by your united disapproval. Now it is time to forgive him and comfort him. Otherwise he may become so bitter and discouraged that he won't be able to recover. Please show him now that you still do love him very much (2:5-8, TLB).

Incredible? Not really. Paul had found a way to triumph amidst tragedy, remain serene amidst perplexity, faithful and loving amidst opposition.

Heaven's Laboratory

The late Dr. Hardy C. Powers used to preach a message from the text, "The steps of a good man are ordered by the Lord" (Ps. 37:23). He would use Rom. 8:28 in conjunction with his thoughts and explain that there is a "laboratory" in heaven. I watched him stir with a circular motion in his imaginary crucible. Into that crucible in the laboratory of heaven would go pain and disappointment, suffering and loss, insult and injury, disillusionment and despair, heartache and woe, bitterness and strife, war and desolation, losses and reverses, spite and maybe even spit; and somehow when God got through mixing it all together with His divine love and mercy, the end result would come out for good. How God does it we will have to be content never to know this side of eternity. "Now we see through a glass, darkly" (1 Cor. 13:12). Any knowledge or understanding will only be partial in life. But someday face-to-face in that encounter with Jesus all the question marks will be erased. For now, we must contend with many things that just don't make sense, and by faith put them into His hands.

Life is full of things that don't make sense. Thank God, though life and people and circumstances put us down, we need not be put out. Vance Havner says, "The way out is not by explanation but by revelation. The Bible does not give us explanation for some of these riddles, but it does supply revelation."[1] It is foolish to assume that the things we cannot understand now, never will be understood. Paul said, "And we know that all that happens to us is working for our good if we love God and are fitting into his plans" (Rom. 8:28, TLB).

The riddles of life must serve to drive us deeper in our faith. If everything made sense, there would be no need to trust God. Vance Havner reminds us that "if everything in life worked out in storybook style we would become complacent and spoiled."[2] Learning to accept the perplexities of life as one of God's methods to bring us to a deeper faith, is the challenge of every Christian. To accept what happens in faith's stride can help us handle all things. The real victory of faith is to trust God in the dark.

"Here, believe. There, understand."

/9

SURVIVAL OF THE FAITHFUL

It does not really matter what causes the locust years of life. When they come, they are brutal, savage, and merciless. Not only do the locusts strike us individually, they have been known to swarm over homes, churches, emotions, morals, denominations, even nations. Just why things happen the way they do will always be difficult to explain, so it seems that a complete understanding of reasons and causes is beyond our grasp. This side of eternity our knowledge and our understanding are now veiled. Facing the fact of an inadequate explanation will remain one of the enduring enigmas of life.

THE WATERGATE EXAMPLE

When America was dragged through the demoralizing experience of the Watergate scandal, many people wondered if the nation could survive. Senators like Charles Percy called the unfolding Watergate disclosures "the darkest scandal in American political history." The issues seemed so grim that the Watergate Committee became committed to following a course aimed at finding the truth at any cost. In Senator Percy's words, "If each kernel of truth must be torn away from those who are hiding it, the effort to redeem our national honor could take years."[1]

The incredible daily revelations, the agonizing hearings brought into our homes through television, successful careers ruined overnight, and the nation's chief executive finally resigning in disgrace led many concerned Americans to wonder if our democracy could survive. Confidence in government and the integrity of national leadership gave way to skepticism and distrust of nearly all public officials. National pride gave way to ignominy and remorse as America's dirty linen was hung out for the world to see.

The Senate Watergate Committee set out with the gargantuan task of redeeming our wounded national honor. Frank Mankiewicz in *Perfectly Clear* states that "countries and societies can survive without a sense of national honor, but cannot long remain free and self-respecting ... The loss of esteem for the system and the honesty and courage of its leaders quickly leads to a loss of self-esteem."[2] This loss of self-esteem and confidence meant a locust year for America, resulting in wounded national pride and fearful division and distrust within the land. In the midst of this devastating and debauching experience many would conclude that our Constitution was an inappropriate document for an advanced nation occupying a whole continent. But as Mankiewicz observed, "It has brought us safe thus far and it is all we have."

It was not until a disgraced president resigned from office in an unprecedented political maneuver and the first invocation of the 25th Amendment occurred that Watergate began to be put behind us. With this began a restoration of national self-respect, and after a while it was again a joy and delight to be an American.

John Dean played a crucial role in the damaging testimony heard at the Senate Watergate hearings. As I watched him and his wife Maureen appear together at the televised hearings, I wonder, looking back now, if this was indeed a locust year in their lives. At some distance from the actual experience of Watergate, Maureen Dean was interviewed by Lois Armstrong of the weekly magazine, *People*. In that enlightening interview, Ms. Armstrong asked Mrs. Dean to comment on the experience of Watergate. She pondered the question and then responded, "It's easy now to say it was worth the pain." Then she made this incredibly profound statement: "Any experience you can survive is worth it."[3]

I doubt that Mrs. Dean really understood the profundity of her words. But something within all of us knows she is absolutely right. As it occurred, America not only survived the dreadful Watergate debacle, but she was morally strengthened, great lessons were learned, and a new push for integrity in government was realized. It happened all because of a locust year that nearly ripped this nation apart at the seams. America survived Watergate and it was worth it.

THE ANDES SURVIVORS

The story of the Andes survivors as reported by Piers Paul Read in his illuminating book, *Alive*, is an incredible saga of the physical and spiritual struggles of the 16 people on an amateur rugby team who overcame one of the most frightening and terrifying ordeals of human endurance ever recorded. Their Fairchild F-227 set off from Montevideo, Uruguay, for Santiago, Chile, on October 12, 1972, carrying an amateur rugby team. Bad weather reported in the Andes Mountains forced them to land in Mendoza, a small town on the Argentinian side of the range. Weather conditions improved the next day, so the Fairchild set off again, flying south. Radio contact with Air Traffic control in Santiago was established at 3:21 p.m. giving their position within the Planchon Pass. Three minutes later the pilot reported that the aircraft was over Curico, Chile, and he was authorized to begin his descent to the Pudahuel airport. At 3:30 p.m. the pilot gave a report on his altitude at 15,000 feet, but a minute later when the control tower spoke in return to the aircraft, there was no answer.[4]

An extensive search was launched lasting eight days, but was finally abandoned because of heavy snowfall in the Andes. Since the roof of the plane was white, there was little hope that the plane would ever be found or that anyone would ever survive. But 10 weeks later, two courageous men who had overcome the most insurmountable obstacles, walked out of the mountains to get help for the other 14 survivors. The account of their survival through every conceivable misfortune is both moving and motivating.

Is any experience you can survive really worth it? The Andes survivors in due time reflected upon their incredible experience. The things that reportedly enabled them to survive were the desire to survive which they refused to abandon, faith in God and continual prayer, the mutual support of a unified group. Most of the survivors agreed that God had given the experience to change them. One of the survivors named Mangino said, "I changed. I know now that I shall be different to what I was . . . all thanks to God." Another named Carlitos Paez said, "Although this experience was sad because of all the friends we lost, it has helped us a lot—in fact it is the greatest experience of my whole life."[5]

When news broke around the world that the survivors had to eat human flesh in order to survive, there came considerable controversy. At a news conference in which the Andes survivors were questioned, Pancho Delgado spoke of the intense loneliness that he felt amidst the majestic surroundings of the snow-capped mountains and the frightening silence which was broken only by the sound of their voices. In the loneliness he felt the presence of God. He said, "I can assure you that God is there. We all felt it, inside ourselves, and not because we were the kind of pious youths who are always praying all day long, not at all. But there one feels the presence of God . . . the hand of God, and allows oneself to be guided by it."[6] At the conclusion of the press conference the public ordeal of the survivors came to an end. It was followed by a long period of adjustment to normal, private life and living. The experience had been excruciating with all the accompanying physical, mental, and spiritual consequences which they would not soon forget. They had survived. Only the years would tell if it was worth it.

SURVIVAL OF THE FAITHFUL

If Maureen Dean is right to say that "any experience you can survive is worth it," then any brush with pain, suffering, sorrow or woe, misunderstanding or despite, that occurs will be worth it if we can somehow come through it. Is it? And what if I do not come through it? It seems that some necessary qualification must be made to her statement. It is not survival of the fittest but rather, survival of the faithful. To put this philosophy of life into a Christian perspective we must add, "Any experience you can survive is worth it if you have faith in God." How then do the faithful survive those times when the locusts swarm and life leaves one crushed and hurt and bleeding? Or what of those things which do not make sense, try as you may to understand why? It is here that God's promise must be accepted with unswerving faith. "I will restore what the locusts have eaten."

Don't Think of It as Punishment

If the faithful survive the locust years, it will be because they have an accurate understanding of God's grace and love. Some immediately ask God when tragedy or a difficult problem strikes, "What have I done to deserve this?" They think of the trouble or tragedy as punishment from God for some wrongdoing or wrongbeing in their life. The so-called comforters of Job tried to convince him, "Job, there is sin in your life. You have done something wrong or else this would not have happened to you." God gave us the Book of Job to refute the notion that suffering comes as punishment from God for sin. Who originated the trouble anyway? Satan! God allowed His servant Job to be tested because He believed in him and no doubt understood Job's point of tolerance.

In the New Testament we are told that God will not put upon us more than we can bear, and will with the temptation or trial, make a way for us to escape (1 Cor. 10:13). James encouraged, "Brothers, as an example of patience in the face of suffering, take the prophets who spoke in the name of the Lord. As you know, we consider blessed those who have persevered. You have heard of Job's perseverance and have seen what the Lord finally brought about. The Lord is full of compassion and mercy" (Jas. 5:10-11, NIV). Job became an example of perseverance, not punishment. So many want to blame God for the troubles and woes of life when Satan ought to be appropriately accused when it is his doing. At one point Jesus said of Peter, "Satan hath desired to . . . sift you as wheat" (Luke 22:31). Satan not only sifted but tried to sink Job. Yet through his fiery ordeal Job came to the place where his faith rose in triumph.

The disciples also mistakenly thought suffering came because of sin when they asked Jesus about the man blind from birth (John 9:2). Jesus' response here indicates that we should not consider tragedy and trouble necessarily as punishment for sin. He said categorically, "Neither hath this man sinned, nor his parents: but that the works of God should be made manifest in him" (v. 3). William Barclay's excellent translation of this verse reads, " . . . it happened that in him there might be a demonstration of what God can do." What a glorious way to view the sufferings and setbacks of life. Here also is an explanation of why God either does not heal or delays His healing. God never does so with vengeance and wrath directed toward people. In His great wisdom and omniscience He may need persons to be a demonstration of what His grace can do for those who trust and rely on Him. God is love. His nature is holy. He gets no hellish glee pulling the rug out from under people.

I once pastored a young man who felt that for every sin and shortcoming on his part, God would respond by throwing some setback or difficulty his way. One of the joys of my life was to help him see that God is no tyrant hurtling tragedy, disappointment, and failure at those who do wrong. Rather, God is a God of love who is doing everything within His power to manifest His love to people individually. We tend to put our own human limitations upon Almighty God. Luther said, "If I were God, I'd knock the world to pieces." But he was not and neither are we. God acts not only for His own sake but for ours. God is not like an absolute monarch who treats each man as a subject to be conquered. God is the Heavenly Father and His way is the way of love. He does not delight in getting our attention by knocking us down. He yearns over us and woos us with His divine, infinite love. "Behold, what manner of love the Father hath bestowed upon us, that we should be called the sons of God" (1 John 3:1). We can face the locust years of life with a confidence in God's grace and love.

REFUSE TO ISOLATE

When you are passing through a locust year experience, it is very easy to see only the darkness and tragedy, to feel only the pain and disappointment of the moment, and forget that God views things from an entirely different perspective. When we isolate the things which stand against us from the full view of an entire life, by themselves they seem unbearable. For example, there are some drugs in which fatal poison is used as a component. Arsenic is a very deadly poison which produces extensive tissue damage and may even cause death. However, when combined with other compounds, such as bismuth, it is highly recommended for the treatment of an intestinal disease. If arsenic were isolated and taken by itself, it would, of course, be fatal. But when mixed with other compounds, it can have a healing effect. The elements of a locust year are like that. Isolated, reduced to the pain of the moment or the troubling circumstance, they are almost unbearable. But given a period of time to be mixed with all the other good things that God does for His children, there can be restoration and healing.

Sometimes we find ourselves looking into the wrong end of a horn of plenty. If you look from the open end into the narrow one, the view is limited. But turn it around and look from the small isolated part outward, the view opens up and gives an entirely different perspective. If we take a locust year experience and isolate it, it may be more than we can take. Our vision is limited to what we can see and feel, and often the pain, tragedy, and disappointment is more than we can bear. It is at times like this we must resolutely refuse to say, "This is all there is." God's view is that of an entire life to be lived. He sees the end from the beginning and understands even all in between. If we refuse to isolate, then before God is through He will bring about restoration and healing. God said it and I believe it: "I will restore . . . [what] the locust hath eaten."

MAINTAIN FAITH

"Without faith it is impossible to please God" (Heb. 11:6). Without faith it is impossible to survive a locust year. In response to one of those "If you can" pleas for help from a demon-possessed boy's father, Jesus said, "Everything is possible for him who believes" (Mark 9:23, NIV). When the locusts are swarming and there is trouble on every hand, the Christian must maintain faith at any cost. America survived Watergate, and history will record that moral integrity was restored when immorality and dishonesty had run its course. The Andes survivors made it because of a will to survive and great faith in God. Faith must tenaciously hold on even when it seems you are dangling by a thread. Restoration is a process which takes place within the context of a vital faith. It is a process described well in a tract entitled *In Times of Trouble*. In times of trouble God's trusting child may cling to four factors in faith.

1. *"He brought me here. It is by His will I am in this difficult place: in that I will rest."* I will maintain faith no matter how tough things become, for I am His child. He owns me. I am His property. I am His responsibility. I am a child of

the King, a joint-heir with Jesus. I may not understand how or why He has allowed me to pass through these things, but I am assured of His infinite love. God loves the world, the lovely and the unlovely; not just one nation; not just the good people. He loves even those who do not love in return. He loves the lonely, those who have messed up their lives, even the ones who never think of God, reject His love, and do not love Him back.

A little girl was playing with her doll in the same room where her mother was busily doing some housework. She knew her mother did not want to be bothered. So when her mother had finished, she told the little girl she could come to her now. The child ran to her, exclaiming, "I'm so glad. I wanted to come to you so much!"

Her mother replied, "But I thought you were happy playing with your doll!"

"Yes, Mother, I was," said the child. "But I soon get tired of loving her, because she can't love me back."

"Is that why you love?" inquired her mother, "just so I can love you back?"

"That's one why," she said, "but not the best one. You loved when I was too little to love you back!"

God never tires of loving us even when we do not love Him in return. "We love him, because he first loved us" (1 John 4:19). If we are assured of His divine love, we can rest in that fact, however difficult the testing ground may be.

2. *"He will keep me here in His love and give me grace in this trial to behave as His child."* God's grace will be sufficient for us and ought to raise us above whining and complaining, no matter how difficult life may be, or how many problems we may have, or how much suffering we endure. God's children behave in such a way that indicates faith. At times, though, we must pray as the

demon-possessed boy's father did, "I do believe; help me overcome my unbelief" (Mark 9:24, NIV).

Paul intimated in his great love chapter (1 Corinthians 13) that our failure to behave as a child of the King nullifies whatever good our suffering may have brought. "If I give all I possess to the poor and surrender my body to the flames, but have not love, I gain nothing" (v. 3, NIV). How tragic to miss God's blessing through suffering because we failed to act or react in love in the midst of our trials and troubles!

God has promised grace and strength to match the trial. When Paul prayed three times for his "thorn in the flesh" to be removed, God said He would not take it away because "My grace is sufficient for thee" (2 Cor. 12:9). That all-sufficient grace includes adequate grace to make us react to whatever our locust years bring, in a way that will not bring discredit to God and His kingdom. "As thy days, so shall thy strength be" (Deut. 33:25).

3. *"He will make the testing a blessing, teaching me the lessons He intends for me to learn, and working in me the grace He intends to give."* One of the dangers of complaining our way through a locust year is that we might miss some of the lessons God is trying to teach us. If we accept the trial and "count it all joy when [we] fall into divers temptations [or trials]," (Jas. 1:2), we are more likely to learn the lessons God intends to teach. The NIV says, "Consider it pure joy, my brothers, whenever you face trials of many kinds, because you know that the testing of your faith develops perseverance. Perseverance must finish its work so that you may be mature and complete, not lacking anything" (vv. 2-4). In other words, there are some things God might be trying to teach us within the trials. If we miss them now, it may take something worse to teach a lesson that should have been learned long before. The choice is ours.

Learn the lessons now or rebel against God's teaching and fail to become what He intends for us to become.

In order for the process of restoration to take place, there must be a proper accompanying attitude. What is this attitude? Simply this: a willingness to learn, a teachable spirit. Jesus said, "It is written in the Prophets: 'They will all be taught by God.' Everyone who listens to the Father and learns from him comes to me" (John 6:45, NIV). It is obvious that God cannot teach the one who feels he has nothing more to learn or whose attitude prevents him from being taught. A disciple of Jesus is a learner. Life is full of hard lessons to be learned. In the face of God's discipline and teaching, be ready to say, "Please be patient, God is not finished with me yet."

4. *"In His good time He can bring me out again—how and when He knows."* [7] One of the most difficult lessons of all to be learned is the discipline of delay. When God gave me the promise of Joel 2:25, I can remember thinking it was a promise that would be fulfilled literally the very next year. When it was not, I had to learn still another difficult lesson: God dictates the process of restoration as well as the duration of it. Even with a promise of restoration in hand and heart, circumstances do not automatically change. To think that God is somehow going to snap His omnipotent fingers and suddenly all the things working against us are going to start working for us, will cause some deep disappointment if we do not remember that God works on His own schedule, not the one we impose upon Him. What should be done after a promise? Wait! In God's good time He will bring us out again; how and when only He knows.

TRY NEVER GIVING UP

Dr. Norman Vincent Peale, in an article with the title of the heading above, suggested that

there are lots of troubles represented among us all and

many . . . are having it hard, finding the going difficult. Sometime you may have the feeling that it is just too much and that you can't quite handle things. When such thoughts come, may I suggest injecting another thought—and it is a powerful thought—try never giving up![8]

The temptation to throw in the towel must be avoided even when it looks like there is no other viable alternative. The survival of the faithful depends largely upon perseverance. "He that endureth to the end shall be saved" (Matt. 10:22). Paul said, "And let us not be weary in well doing: for in due season we shall reap, if we faint not" (Gal. 6:9). These are but a few of God's promises to those who refuse to give up.

It is most easy to become weary in doing good things. Pastors and Christian workers are most susceptible to this. A good rule to remember when we are prone to feelings of failure over meager results after maximum effort is this: "Do your best and leave the rest." Most of us have the wrong idea about our own success. So come out from under the juniper tree, quit feeling sorry for yourself, and try never giving up. God's promise is: "He that goeth forth and weepeth, bearing precious seed, shall doubtless come again with rejoicing, bringing his sheaves with him" (Ps. 126:6). The victory is in never giving up, never conceding defeat even though you may feel down. Paul said, "We get knocked down, but we get up again and keep going" (2 Cor. 4:9, TLB). There is a difference. So Paul could say, "Therefore, since through God's mercy we have this ministry, we do not lose heart" (2 Cor. 4:1, NIV).

Once Eddie Rickenbacker was in an airplane crash at Atlanta and was rushed to a hospital. It was thought that his injuries would surely cause death. He was in and out of consciousness for a while. One radio commentator at the time said in a broadcast, "Friends, pray for Eddie Rickenbacker. He is dying in an Atlanta hospital. He is not expected to live out the night." Rickenbacker was listening to the radio; and when he heard this remark, he took a jug of water from his bedside and threw it at the radio, knocking it across the room, thus stopping the voice announcing that he was dying. He said, "I'm not going to die. I'm not going to give up."⁹ That is the spirit of a man who desires to survive: never give up. When all else fails, why not try never giving up?

James J. Corbett became the heavyweight boxing champion of the world half a century or so ago. The quality of perseverance took him to the top of his profession as indicated by one of his statements:

> Fight one more round. When your feet are so tired that you shuffle back to the center of the ring, fight one more round.
>
> When your arms are so tired that you can hardly lift your hands to come on guard, fight one more round. When your nose is bleeding, and your eyes are black, and you are so tired that you wish your opponent would crack you one on the jaw and put you to sleep, fight one more round—remembering that the man who always fights one more round is never whipped.[10]

We are whipped when we quit, so we must determine never to give up.

Live Dangerously Faithful

Gerald Kennedy tells in a recorded sermon of a resistance fighter in France in 1941. He was facing the invasion of his land. Tyranny had come in, and it looked hopeless for a long time ahead. What should he do? Come to terms with the tyrant? That is what a good many were doing. Or should he join the underground movement and risk his life? In that moment of crucial decision he wrote these words: "This is not a time for me to desert my faith. It is not a time to turn for new images for my belief. This is the time for me to be dangerously faithful."[11]

In the words of this resistance fighter there is a message for anyone who will ever face a locust year in life. Determine to be dangerously faithful. Paul caught the spirit well when he wrote, "Stand firm. Let nothing move you. Always give yourselves fully to the work of the Lord, because you know that your labor in the Lord is not in vain" (1 Cor. 15:58, NIV). Giving God the time He needs to bring us through will help us to be dangerously faithful amidst circumstances less than encouraging—dangerously faithful in spite of pressures which push us to depression—dangerously faithful because God is still God. Remember, it is not the fittest but the dangerously faithful who will survive the locust years of life.

Reference Notes

CHAPTER 1:
1. From the song "He Giveth More Grace," by Annie Johnson Flint. Copyright 1941. Renewed 1969 by Lillenas Publishing Co.
2. John Newton, "Amazing Grace," in *Worship in Song*, No. 212.
3. Will T. Thompson, "Jesus Is All the World to Me," in *Worship in Song*, No. 367.

CHAPTER 2:
1. John M. Drescher, *Follow Me* (Scottdale, Pa.: Herald Press, 1971), p. 66.
2. *Ibid.*, p. 67.
3. Harold Lindsell, *The World, the Flesh, and the Devil* (Washington: Canon Press, 1973), p. 37.
4. *Ibid.*, p. 45.
5. *Ibid.*, p. 46.
6. *Ibid.*, p. 38.
7. William Barclay, *The Revelation of John* (Philadelphia: The Westminster Press, 1959), 1:113.
8. James Dobson, *Hide or Seek* (Old Tappan, N.J.: Fleming H. Revell Co., 1974), p. 17.

CHAPTER 3:
1. Reuben Welch, *When You Run out of Fantastic—Persevere* (Nashville: Impact Books, 1976).
2. Barclay, *The Revelation of John*, 1:93-95.

CHAPTER 4:
1. Paul Tournier, trans. by Helen & John Doberstein, *The Whole Person in a Broken World* (New York: Harper and Row Publishers, 1964), p. 2.
2. Paul J. Gillette and Marie Hornbeck, *Depression: A Layman's Guide* (New York: Outerbridge and Fazard, Inc., 1973), p. 16.
3. Tournier, *The Whole Person*, p. 21.
4. *Ibid.*, p. 8.
5. *Ibid.*, pp. 24-25.
6. *Ibid.*, p. 25.
7. *Ibid.*

8. O. Quentin Hyder, M.D., *The Christian's Handbook of Psychiatry* (Old Tappan, N.J.: Fleming H. Revell Co., 1971), p. 47.

9. *Ibid.*, p. 69.

10. *Ibid.*, p. 47.

11. William B. Terhune, M.D., *Mastering Your Emotions* (New York: William Morrow Co., Inc., 1970), p. 20.

12. *Ibid.*, p. 21.

13. *Ibid.*, p. 24.

14. Rolland S. Parker, *Emotional Common Sense* (New York: Harper and Row Publishers, 1973), p. 54.

15. *Ibid.*

16. Hyder, *Christian's Handbook*, p. 106.

17. *Ibid.*

18. Parker, *Common Sense*, p. 54.

19. See Parker, *Common Sense*, pp. 58-59 for an in-depth look at the sources of stress.

20. Cited in Gillette, *Depression*, pp. 16-17.

21. *Ibid.*

22. Leonard Cammer, M.D., *Up from Depression* (New York: Simon and Schuster, 1969), p. 16.

23. *Ibid.*

24. Parker, *Common Sense*, p. 61.

25. Cammer, *Depression*, p. 16

26. Clifton E. & Clinton J. Kew, *You Can Be Healed* (New York: Prentice-Hall, Inc., 1953), p. 165.

27. Hyder, *Christian's Handbook*, p. 85.

28. Parker, *Common Sense*, p. 80.

29. Cecil Osborne, *Release from Fear and Anxiety* (Waco: Word Books, Inc., 1976), p. 19.

30. Earl Lee, *The Cycle of Victorious Living* (Kansas City: Beacon Hill Press of Kansas City, 1971), p. 18.

31. *Ibid.*

32. Terhune, *Mastering Your Emotions*, p. 15.

33. Vivian A. Kretz, "Thou Wilt Keep Him in Perfect Peace," in *Worship in Song* (Kansas City: Lillenas Publishing Co., 1972), No. 419.

CHAPTER 5:

1. Edward Shorter, *The Making of the Modern Family* (New York: Basic Books, Inc., 1975), p. 269.

2. Thomas C. McGinnis and John U. Agus, *Open Family Living* (New York: Doubleday & Co., Inc., 1976), pp. 12-13.

3. Shorter, *Modern Family*, p. 4.
4. Quoted from *St. Louis Post-Dispatch* article by Philip Sutin.
5. *Ibid.*
6. Furnished by Fingertip Facts, Crown National Bureau.
7. Fingertip Facts, quoted from *Newsweek*, Oct. 10, 1977.
8. Pitirim A. Sorokin, *The American Sex Revolution* (Boston: Porter Sargent Publisher, 1956), p. 3.
9. Vance Packard, *The Sexual Wilderness* (New York: David McKay Co., Inc., 1968), p. 17.
10. *Ibid.*, p. 13.
11. Sorokin, *Sex Revolution*, p. 12.
12. Cited in Packard, *Sexual Wilderness*, p. 9.
13. Sorokin, *Sex Revolution*, p. 19.
14. *Ibid.*, p. 14.
15. *Ibid.*, p. 76.
16. Packard, *Sexual Wilderness*, p. 77.
17. *Ibid.*
18. *Ibid.*, p. 14.
19. Alvin Toffler, *Future Shock* (New York: Random House, 1970), p. 222.
20. "Today" show, Feb. 27, 1969.
21. Jo Carr and Imogene Sorley, *The Intentional Family* (Nashville: Abingdon Press, 1971), p. 121.
22. Cited in Packard, *Sexual Wilderness*, p. 22.
23. *Ibid.*
24. Carr and Sorley, *The Intentional Family*, p. 122.
25. Cited in Packard, *Sexual Wilderness*, p. 23.
26. Carr and Sorley, *The Intentional Family*, p. 122.
27. Betty Yoburg, *The Changing Family* (New York: Columbia University Press, 1973), p. 190.
28. *Ibid.*, p. 191.
29. Fingertip Facts, *Newsweek*, Oct. 10, 1977.
30. Yoburg, *Changing Family*, p. 190.
31. Carr and Sorley, *Intentional Family*, p. 120.

CHAPTER 6:
1. Michael P. Hamilton, *The Charismatic Movement* (Grand Rapids: William B. Eerdmans Publishing Co., 1975), p. 7.
2. John Sherrill, *They Speak with Other Tongues* (New York: Grune & Stratton, 1970), p. 133.
3. James C. Logan, "Controversial Aspects of the Movement," in *The Charismatic Movement*, p. 33.

4. Cited in Donald W. Burdick, *Tongues: To Speak or Not to Speak* (Chicago: Moody Press, 1969), p. 84.
5. Logan, *Charismatic Movement*, p. 35.
6. *Ibid.*, p. 37.
7. Burdick, *Tongues: To Speak or Not to Speak*, p. 84.
8. Cited in John M. Drescher, *Follow Me* (Scottdale, Pa.: Herald Press, 1971), p. 14.
9. Logan, *Charismatic Movement*, p. 39.
10. Cited in Wesley L. Duewel, *The Holy Spirit and Tongues* (Winona Lake, Ind.: Light and Life Press, 1974), p. 80.
11. *Ibid.*, p. 82.
12. Cited in Burdick, *Tongues*, p. 69.
13. Cited in Duewel, *Holy Spirit*, p. 93.
14. *Ibid.*

CHAPTER 7:
1. "AMA Is Urging Firms to Stop Sponsoring Violent TV Shows," *St. Louis Post-Dispatch*, Feb. 7, 1977.
2. *Ibid.*
3. Don Jamieson, *The Troubled Air* (Fredericton, N.B.: Brunswick Press, 1966), p. 9.
4. *Ibid.*, pp. 9-10.
5. Subcommittee on Communication of the Committee on Commerce, *Federal Communication Committee Policy Matters and TV Programming: A Hearing*, U.S. Congress, Senate, 91st Cong., 1st sess. (Washington, D.C.: U.S. Government Printing Office, 1969), p. 409.
6. *Ibid.*, p. 338.
7. David A. Seamands, *Problem Solving in the Christian Family* (Carol Stream, Ill.: Creation House, 1975), p. 14.
8. William Y. Elliott, *Television's Impact on American Culture* (East Lansing, Mich.: Michigan State University Press, 1956), p. 17.
9. *Ibid.*, p. 15.
10. William P. Dizard, *Television: A World View* (Syracuse, N.Y.: Syracuse University Press, 1966), p. 1.
11. *Ibid.*
12. *Ibid.*, p. 2.
13. *Ibid.*, p. 3.
14. Harry J. Skornia, *Television and Society* (New York: McGraw-Hill Publishing Co., 1965), p. 148.
15. *Ibid.*, p. 143.
16. *Ibid.*, pp. 149-50.

17. Dizard, *Television*, p. 165.
18. Seamands, *Problem Solving*, p. 14.
19. Quoted in Charleston newspaper editorial entitled, "TV Crime," Jan. 1, 1975.
20. Letters to the Editor, Charleston newspaper, Mrs. Patricia A. Mitchum commenting, Jan. 19, 1975.
21. "TV Crime," Jan. 1, 1975.
22. "TVs to Be Turned Off in Protest over Violence," *St. Louis Post-Dispatch*, Feb. 18, 1977.
23. *Ibid.*
24. "Birth Control Is Taught in Some Area Classrooms," *St. Louis Post-Dispatch*, Mar. 3, 1977.

CHAPTER 8:
1. Vance Havner, *Hearts Afire* (Old Tappan, N.J.: Fleming H. Revell Co., 1952), p. 46.
2. *Ibid.*, p. 48.

CHAPTER 9:
1. Frank Mankiewicz, *Perfectly Clear* (NYT Quadrangle: The New York Times Book Co., 1973), p. 189.
2. *Ibid.*
3. Lois Armstrong, *People* Magazine (Chicago: Time, Inc., 1976), p. 31.
4. Piers Paul Read, *Alive* (New York: Avon Books, 1974), p. 13.
5. *Ibid.*, p. 291.
6. *Ibid.*, pp. 305-6.
7. Quoted from *Silent Evangelist*, No. 176 (Grand Rapids: Faith, Prayer, and Tract League).
8. Norman Vincent Peale, "Try Never Giving Up," in *Creative Help for Daily Living* (Pawling, N.Y.: Foundation for Christian Living, 1978), p. 26.
9. *Ibid.*, pp. 27-28.
10. Wilbur E. Nelson, *Anecdotes and Illustrations* (Grand Rapids: Baker Book House, 1971), p. 96.
11. Gerald Kennedy, "Dangerously Faithful" (A cassette tape) (Waco: Word, Inc., 1977).